Triumphs Amidst Trials

OrangeBooks Publication

1st Floor, Rajhans Arcade, Mall Road, Kohka, Bhilai, Chhattisgarh 490020

Website: **www.orangebooks.in**

© Copyright, 2024, Author

All rights reserved. No part of this book may be reproduced, stored in a retrieval system, or transmitted, in any form by any means, electronic, mechanical, magnetic, optical, chemical, manual, photocopying, recording or otherwise, without the prior written consent of its writer.

First Edition, 2024

Triumphs AMIDST Trials

MOHIT GOEL

OrangeBooks Publication
www.orangebooks.in

NEVER GIVE UP!

YOU ARE NOT ALONE!

Preface

There comes a time in life where, in certain circumstances, it seems that there is no way out. At that moment, your mind and body start to give up, and you feel like running away from reality. It happens to all of us, and there is nothing to be ashamed of or feel embarrassed about in accepting that you are in a difficult situation for which you need a way out, either by yourself or with somebody's help.

This incident happened in my life back in 2015. I had just completed my studies and joined my father's business. I was new to the business then and started learning how it works, but suddenly, after a few months, my father got diagnosed with cancer and passed away in 6 months. I could have given up, but my mother was there to support my family and help me out in the business. But after two years, my mother also passed away.

At that time, when my father and mother were in hospital getting their treatment, I started thinking that there must be many people like me in the world who face similar situations in their life and have nobody by their side to share the pain or to motivate them, telling them that life is not over. There is no need to give up. I was fortunate enough to have my family and friends by my side. Unfortunately, not everyone has a support system.

So, I started looking on the internet and searching for people who have also faced setbacks in life but overcame them with a never-give-up attitude. I was amazed to see that almost all the successful celebrities, sports personalities, industrialists, political leaders, etc., have faced a setback once in their lives. That setback has helped them to achieve great things in life.

Never Give Up (Volume 1) book is a part of Project Never Give Up. The primary goal is to inspire and motivate individuals, offering hope, faith, and love through the sharing of such stories. All the stories are kept short to carry the book with you all the time and flip through its pages whenever you feel like giving up.

By buying this, you will not be helping only yourself but others. All the profit from this book's sale will be donated to various NGOs working towards Cancer Research, helping the elderly, providing food to the poor, etc. You can find the list of all the NGOs in the book's last section.

To Dad and Mom

Introduction

The book 'Never Give Up' is a manuscript – a project meant to inspire and motivate people. The hope is that your spirit will be lifted when you flip through it, and you will realize there is no reason to give up in life.

It's a hard process, we know. But together, we can accomplish greatness.

This book is a collection of inspiring stories about famous people. How did their life start? What did they have to push through? How did they survive?

They were once ordinary, neutral, and normal like every other person who roamed the earth. Their desire to make changes kept burning in their hearts, which is how they nurtured their ideas. Their ideas inspired their ways and made them enthusiastic about life. We hope you will find solace, life, and knowledge in their history. And also that the story of these people, who have grown to be colourful rainbows, will challenge you to keep on fighting and never let the fire die.

LIVE ON. NEVER GIVE UP.

Contents

Soichiro Honda – Failed 99% Of The Time Before Success 1

How To Win When Circumstances Are Unfavourable 5

Elizabeth Arden – The Inspiration For Hardworking And Confidence 8

How To Cope With Disappointment 11

Mark Cuban – The Brain Of Business 15

Katy Perry 21

How To Succeed In Life 24

Bill Gates – The Team Maker! 27

Bethany Hamilton: The One-Armed Professional Surfer. 35

5 Ways To Make Your Dreams Come True 40

Jim Carrey: Story Of Endurance 43

Walt Disney: Tasted Failure But Didn't Give Up 51

5 Ways Not To Give Up On Your Dream 58

J.K. Rowling – All About Her Inspiring World 62

Stephen King – The Perseverance Hero 68

6 Ways To Be Successful In Life 72

Oprah Winfrey – Suffered But Thrived At Last 76

Sylvester Stallone - Journey In Bringing Rocky To
Life And His Success 82

8 Ways To Remain Committed To Your Dreams
After Emotional Abuse 86

Steven Spielberg – The Heartbreaking And Inspiring Story Of
The Greatest Movie Maker Of All Time 90

Jay-Z's Story Gives Hope To The Hardworking 99

Dr A.P.J Abdul Kalam: A Model Of Dedication And
Contribution 104

5 Ways You Can Turn Failure Into Success 109

Henry Ford: From Scratch To The Pinnacle Of
The Auto Industry 112

5 Tips To Focus On Your Dream 116

Harrison Ford: Crafting Wealth From Sheer Skill 118

Michael Jordan: The Tale Of An Iconic Legend 123

5 Ways To Manage Your Time In Career Development 127

Abraham Lincoln: The Embodiment Of Resilience
And Tenacity 130

Steve Jobs: The Embodiment Of
Technological Brilliance 134

Goal-Setting Workbook: Transforming Inspiration
Into Action 139

Your Journey, Your Story: Embracing Life's
Challenges With Resilience 144

List Of Ngo's 148

References 150

Soichiro Honda – Failed 99% of the Time Before Success

"Many people dream of success. To me, success can only be achieved through repeated failure and introspection."

Honda is one of the most well-known motor companies in the world. However, you may not have given much thought to how they came to be in business in the first place. It is a really interesting story, not least because of the obstacles that Soichiro Honda had to overcome in order to found the company. The story highlights how you need to be prepared to overcome failure to enjoy success.

Honda's dream was to work for Toyota, Japan's biggest engineering firm at that time. However, he was only 15 years old and had no formal education. He left home and moved closer to where Toyota was based.

Years passed, and he eventually got married and managed to rent a small workshop where he developed an engine piston ring, which was revolutionary at the time. He sometimes spent whole days in his workshop and even slept there overnight. He also sold some of his wife's jewellery to raise money for his work. When he presented it to Toyota, though, he was told that it did not meet their high engineering standards.

This was a personal disappointment, but Honda did not give up. He enrolled in a technical school to get more experience and find out what his piston ring lacked in terms of engineering. It took another two years, but he finally created a product that Toyota was happy with. The piston rings could be used for aeroplanes, cars, and motorcycles, and Honda was offered a contract to make these. He knew that he needed a factory rather than a workshop, but the timing could not have been worse. The year was 1941, and Japan was preparing to go to war with the United States. The materials that Honda needed to build his factory just weren't available.

This led to him inventing a whole new process for making concrete. He was able to use the concrete he made to build his factory.

Just as it looked like things were finally going his way, his factory was almost destroyed when it was bombed twice during the war. He was unable to rebuild because even though he had resolved the concrete problem, the steel he needed was all being used to produce armaments. However, Honda was not about to give in just yet.

Members of the US Air Force often threw away gasoline cans after they were empty. Honda collected as many of these cans as he could, and remarkably, he was able to collect enough to melt down and produce the steel he needed to rebuild his factory. By 1945, the factory had been rebuilt, and the Second World War was all but over. But unbelievably, disaster struck again: an earthquake occurred, and the factory was destroyed for the third time. He knew he could not rebuild his factory again, so he decided to cut his losses and sell his manufacturing processes to Toyota. He thought that his dream of owning his own business had finally ended.

The Reinvention Of Honda

The war had left a huge shortage of fuel in Japan. This made it very difficult for people to travel around. Trains were used for long journeys, and people rode bikes for short trips. Honda did not like seeing what Japan had become and wanted to do something to help people try and get their lives back to normal. He had the idea of putting a motor on his bike to travel faster and further than if he were pedalling. The motorised bicycle proved very popular, and his friends soon began to ask if he could make one for them as well. Without even trying, he ended up being back in business.

However, he still had the issue of not being able to afford to build a factory. He knew that he would need to find people willing to invest in his business. This was not going to be easy when there were not many people in the country who had any money to invest. But Honda was nothing if not determined, and he wrote an estimated 18,000 letters to bicycle shop owners all over the country to see if they would be interested in his invention and if they could put up some capital to make it happen. This would have involved him writing out 18,000 individual letters and sending them out by post, showing that he never lost any of his determination to succeed.

From these letters, he received 3000 positive responses from shop owners who were interested to find out more about these 'scooters', and if selling them would help to grow their business. Honda soon got the money he needed to start producing these bicycles.

Today, the company Honda is the largest producer of motorcycles in the world. It has factories worldwide, and as of 2022, Honda employs more than 200,000 people[1]. The revenue of the company is around $10 billion per year. None of this would have been possible if not for the determination of Soichiro Honda. There were so many points of his journey where it would have been far easier to give up than to carry on. It took 17 years from the point where he was working in his small workshop to starting to sell his first motorized bicycles.

You cannot help but be inspired by Honda's story and his refusal to give up on his dream. It just goes to show what can be achieved when you believe in yourself and what you can accomplish.

How to Win When Circumstances Are Unfavourable

1. **Make A List Of Your Exact Objectives**

The situation is like running a race without knowing where the finish line is. Can you see yourself coming out on top? Doubtless not. That's why having a clear goal in mind and knowing where you stand concerning it is essential. And instead of aimlessly toiling away, train yourself to work towards a goal.

2. **Cultivate A Sense Of Accountability**

One must not make excuses or place blame on others. Successful people know they are responsible for their own downfall and accept the consequences of their actions. In contrast to losers, winners actively seek out ways to overcome obstacles.

3. Develop A Routine That Consistently Benefits You

Sounds weird, right? Unfortunately, you'll need to take that step. Developing a habit that will bring you success is challenging. To develop a habit of success, you must alter your perspective and view obstacles as opportunities. Every day, force yourself to do something you couldn't do before, and you'll develop the habit of pushing yourself.

4. Don't Give In To Fear

You shouldn't be afraid to fail. Accepting your mistakes as learning opportunities is the best course of action. Don't let setbacks discourage you. Take full advantage of it. That's what you learned, and that's what you should use to your advantage the next time.

5. Learn Something New Every Day

Learn something new, read something interesting, talk to someone new, or try something exciting every day since acquiring more information increases one's chances of success in life.

6. Don't Be Afraid To Take Risks

It is important not to let fear prevent you from trying new things because being overly cautious can cause you to miss an opportunity, and you may never get a second chance at it.

7. Stay Focused

Keep your sights set on the goal. Don't let your mind wander; stay diligent and committed. Simply put, you are not taking anything seriously if you are not fully present in the moment. You can't succeed in life if you don't take it seriously.

8. The Willingness To Put In Extra Effort Is Essential

Working hard is the key to success. If your rival regularly performs 200 push-ups, you should aim to do 300 to remain competitive. It's important to remember that the more work you put in, the better the rewards will be, and this is true in all areas of life, not just sports.

Exercise For You

Risk-Taking Exercise

Identify an opportunity or challenge you've been hesitant to pursue due to fear. Develop a small, manageable plan to address this fear and take a calculated risk. Reflect on the experience and the lessons learned, aligning with Honda's resilience in the face of adversity.

Elizabeth Arden – The Inspiration For Hardworking And Confidence

"Repetition makes reputation and reputation makes customers."

Elizabeth Arden was a Canadian - American business woman who founded the Elizabeth Arden Inc. fragrance brand. She worked hard to build this cosmetic empire at a time when men often dominated the world of business.

She was born Florence Nightingale Graham on December 31st, 1884[2]. She was one of five children, and her family lived in Woodbridge, Ontario, Canada. They had little money, and Elizabeth took on odd jobs to bring more money into the home. After she left school, she studied nursing and worked a lot with patients who had been burned. She became interested in the lotions used to treat burns, which was her first step towards becoming a successful businesswoman.

However, her journey in business was not an easy one. Her first attempts to get her business off the ground all failed. She partnered with Elizabeth Hubbard, but this business only lasted six months before failing. These failures only made her more determined to succeed, and she reinvented herself with the name Elizabeth Arden. By this time, she was living in New York City, and this is where she opened her Red Door Salon[3]. It was from these humble beginnings that her empire grew.

Once her business finally started to get off the ground, there was no looking back. Her empire of salons continued growing until she had more than 150 salons across the United States and Europe. She developed and sold more than 1,000 product lines in 22 different countries. Her hard work and passion for her business played a large part in her success. At one point, Elizabeth Arden Inc. was making $1 billion in annual sales[4]. This made her one of the wealthiest women in the world. Even today, hers is still considered one of the most successful beauty businesses of all time.

What Life Lessons Can Be Learned from Elizabeth Arden?

One of the main things that can be learned from Elizabeth Arden's story is the importance of never giving up. Even when things were not going well, she remained passionate about following her dreams. If you believe in yourself and have confidence that you will achieve what you want to, then success will come. Failure is a part of life and almost to be expected, but it only becomes a real failure if it causes you to give up.

What Are Some of Elizabeth Arden's Most Famous Inventions?

Elizabeth Arden is widely recognized as the person who brought eye makeup to the United States. The modern concept of a "make-over" was also one of her innovations. She developed travel-sized beauty products so women could take their favourite products wherever they went.

What Brands Are Owned by Elizabeth Arden, Inc.?

Elizabeth Arden Inc. owns many other fragrance and cosmetic brands, although a lot of people don't realise it. These include fragrances by Britney Spears, Mariah Carey, and Hilary Duff[5].

How To Cope With Disappointment

It is not always easy to cope with disappointment, especially if the situation is not expected. Unfortunately, disappointment is something that we all have to face at one time or another. There are things you can do, though, that can help you deal with things. Some of these tricks are described in more detail below.

1. Get To Know Disappointment

Disappointment is the feeling you get when things don't work out as you hoped. It can manifest in a number of different ways. You may experience feelings of sadness, hopelessness, anger, or even a mixture of all three.

You need to remember that it is natural to feel the way you do. Giving yourself a hard time about how you are feeling will only make the situation worse. Once you have accepted these feelings, it will be easier to move on from them.

2. Give Yourself Time To Reflect

Give yourself time to reflect on the situation, and think about why things turned out the way they did.

It may be that the situation took you completely by surprise, or it may be that there were signs that things were going to go wrong.

If you can learn from this experience, you will be better equipped to deal with any disappointments in the future.

3. Change Your Outlook

While you can be disappointed with a particular outcome, this may work out for the best in the long run.

Try to focus not on your disappointment but on things you can change. It may be that you need to alter your expectations slightly.

If this is something you are actively trying to do, try to ensure you are working through the feelings of disappointment rather than just trying to forget it happened.

4. Don't Dwell On Your Disappointment

If you are disappointed about a certain situation, it can be easy to wallow in this disappointment. However, this makes it more difficult for you to move on.

It can be more productive for you to focus on the positives of the experience. Think about if there were things that worked well and what you would do differently next time around.

5. **Take Care Of Yourself**

Always ensure that you are taking good care of yourself. If you are not feeling your best, then it can be hard to concentrate on self-care.

However, you will feel much less stressed if you ensure you eat properly and get enough rest. This will make it easier for you to move on from and deal with your feelings of disappointment.

Exercises For You

The Repetition Challenge

Develop a personal or professional skill through consistent practice, emphasizing the principle "Repetition makes reputation." Elizabeth Arden's quote underscores the significance of consistent effort. Choose a skill, be it related to your career or personal growth, and commit to daily practice. Track your progress and note how repetition enhances your competence over time. Reflect on the journey, considering how dedication and repetition contribute to skill development.

The Billion-Dollar Vision

Outline a visionary goal or project you aspire to achieve. Break down the goal into actionable steps and create a roadmap for its execution. Elizabeth Arden's empire reached extraordinary heights, emphasizing the power of visionary thinking. Apply this concept to your own life by setting a grand goal. Break it down into manageable tasks, creating a timeline for completion. Regularly review your progress, and celebrate milestones achieved. This challenge encourages long-term planning and sustained effort.

Mark Cuban – The Brain Of Business

"It doesn't matter how many times you fail. You only have to be right once and then everyone can tell you that you are an overnight success."

Mark Cuban, widely recognized for his exceptional leadership abilities, fearless expression of opinions, and remarkable entrepreneurial skills, has made an enduring impact on business. Hailing from a family of refugees in Pittsburgh, Pennsylvania, Cuban's formative years were shaped by unwavering determination and drive to achieve greatness. From humble beginnings, he became a beacon of inspiration, proving that anyone can overcome obstacles and achieve greatness with determination and the right opportunities.

Early Life

In 1958, Mark Cuban entered the world as a member of a Jewish immigrant family hailing from Russia[6]. His grandfather and father worked tirelessly to provide for their family, instilling in Cuban the values of hard work and perseverance. Despite facing challenging circumstances, Cuban refused to succumb to adversity. During these formative years, he discovered his sense of purpose, realizing that the key to a fulfilling life lies in seizing opportunities and pushing beyond perceived limitations.

Cuban's education began at Mount Lebanon High School in Pennsylvania, where he received academic instruction and gained practical skills through various part-time jobs. Even at the tender age of 12, Cuban exhibited an enterprising spirit by selling a pair of shoes, an early indication of his business acumen[7]. This early experience taught him the importance of recognizing potential opportunities and propelled him toward a future of entrepreneurial success.

Life After Graduation

Following his graduation from Indiana University of Bloomington, Mark Cuban embarked on a new chapter in his life. At first, he returned to his beloved hometown of Pittsburgh and obtained employment at a bank. Nevertheless, Cuban's ambitions transcended the boundaries of his familiar surroundings, and he longed for boundless prospects. In 1982, he took a daring leap and departed from Pittsburgh, redirecting his path toward Dallas[8]-a consequential choice that would forever reshape the course of his existence.

Armed with the fundamentals he had acquired during his education, Cuban was determined to transform his dreams into reality. He understood the importance of laying a strong foundation before starting his entrepreneurial journey. This approach underscored his unwavering commitment to his vision. In pursuing one's aspirations, it becomes imperative to dedicate time to comprehending the fundamentals and crafting a robust strategy. Through this deliberate approach, Cuban positioned himself for enduring triumph and served as a model for those who would follow suit.

Upon arriving in Dallas, Cuban initially found work in a software company, where he honed his skills and gained valuable industry experience. However, his entrepreneurial spirit continued to drive him forward, eventually leading him to establish his consulting business, "MicroSolutions." Cuban's unique perspective on computers and software propelled his business to rapid success. In 1990, he made a groundbreaking deal by selling MicroSolutions to CompuServe for a staggering sum of $6 million[9]. This achievement marked a significant milestone in his career, showcasing his ability to identify opportunities and execute profitable ventures.

Undeterred by his previous success, Cuban embarked on another entrepreneurial endeavour in 1995. Alongside his partner Todd Wagner, he founded "AudioNet," later known as Broadcast.com. This pioneering internet radio company revolutionized how people consumed media online. Cuban's relentless drive and innovative thinking propelled the company to unprecedented heights. In 1999, Broadcast.com caught the attention of Yahoo!, leading to a remarkable acquisition worth nearly $6 billion[9]. These achievements solidified Cuban's status as a business visionary and confirmed his ability to navigate the dynamic landscape of technology and media.

Before reaching his notable success, Mark Cuban faced numerous challenges and setbacks. There were moments when he returned home to find the power shut off due to unpaid bills. However, instead of succumbing to negativity, Cuban used these difficulties as motivation to overcome obstacles and propel himself forward. His resilience and unwavering determination serve as a reminder that turning adversity into motivation can lead to greater achievements in life.

Accomplishments

The achievements of Mark Cuban in both the business and sports arenas stand as a testament to his unwavering determination and forward-thinking mentality. Building upon his entrepreneurial triumphs, he boldly delved into sports ownership, leaving an indelible mark on the basketball landscape. In a daring manoeuvre in 2000, Cuban embarked on a transformative journey by acquiring the Dallas Mavericks, an NBA franchise that had grappled with achieving prosperity. Determined to turn the franchise around, he brought his passion and dedication to the team, transforming their fortunes.

Under Cuban's ownership, the Dallas Mavericks experienced a remarkable turnaround. With his hands-on approach and an unyielding dedication to achieving greatness, he fostered a culture of triumph within the organization. The Mavericks soared to unprecedented heights through Cuban's exceptional leadership and astute decision-making, emerging as a formidable powerhouse within the NBA.

In addition to his sports endeavours, Mark Cuban expanded his influence in the media industry. In 2001, he co-founded the high-definition television network HDNet alongside Philip Garvin. HDNet distinguished itself by providing the highest level of digital broadcast quality, revolutionizing the television viewing experience. Cuban's innovation and foresight in the media landscape further showcased his ability to identify and capitalize on emerging trends[10].

Furthermore, Cuban established the media company '2929' with his former partner, Todd Wagner. Through this venture, Cuban continued to make waves in the entertainment industry. '2929' encompassed various branches, including film production, distribution, and exhibition[11]. Cuban's engagement in the media sector reinforced his standing as a versatile entrepreneur capable of leaving a profound imprint on diverse industries.

Exercise For You

Personal Accomplishments Journal:

Create a journal documenting your personal accomplishments, both big and small. Regularly update it with your achievements, lessons learned, and goals for the future. Reflect on how maintaining this journal impacts your mindset and motivation, drawing inspiration from Mark Cuban's relentless drive.

Katy Perry

"If you can believe in something great, then you can achieve something great."

Katy Perry had a very strict religious upbringing. This surprises many people because of how she dresses now and the content of her songs. Her parents were pastors, and the only music she could listen to was gospel music[12].

Music channels MTV and VH1 were banned in the house, and Katy could only listen to pop music if her friends lent her their CDs.

Despite not having much access to music, it soon became obvious that she was a talented singer. Her parents enrolled her in singing lessons, and she began performing in church at 9. She received a guitar as a birthday present when she was 13, and she soon began to write and perform her own songs.

During her teenage years, she started to rebel against the strict upbringing she had received. She began to get more experimental with her music and even got a nose piercing.

In 2001, she moved from Santa Barbara to Nashville, hoping to launch a successful music career. She released an album of gospel music called Katy Hudson, the name she was christened with. She later started to use the professional name Katy Perry, as Perry was her mother's maiden name. This album was never a success because the label went bankrupt soon after its release[13].

However, despite this disappointment, Perry was not ready to give up on her music career just yet. After finishing high school, she moved to Los Angeles, where she worked with Glen Ballard, a songwriter and producer. He had previously worked with stars such as Christina Aguilera.

She has described this as a difficult time in her life because she was only 17 then, and it was the first time she had ever lived alone. She needed to find other jobs away from music to help her to pay the bills.

Between 2004 and 2007, three record deals fell through before she could sign them. There must have been a point where she thought that things would never work out for her, but then she signed a deal with Capitol Records in 2007.

She released her first single, "Ur So Gay", with the label, but it was not an instant success. It caught the attention of Madonna, who called it her favourite song of the moment, but it did not do that well in the charts.

All this changed with the release of her second single, "I Kissed A Girl". This went straight to the top of the charts, and when she released her first album with Capitol, it went straight into the top 10.

From this point, she has not really looked back on her music career. She has also started to move into acting, appearing in The Simpsons and How I Met Your Mother. She was also the voice of Smurfette in the Smurfs movies. In 2021, she began her residency at Resorts World Las Vegas, following in the footsteps of musical icons such as Britney Spears, Celine Dion, and Elton John, who have all had residencies in Vegas.

Accomplishment

Perry has won American Music Awards, People's Choice Awards, Billboard Music Awards, Guinness World Records, Brits Award, and Juno Award. In September 2012, The Bulletin named her the "Woman of the Year."[14]

She has made four Guinness World Records – Best Start on the US Digital Chart by a Female Artist, First Female with Five Number One US singles from One Album, Most Twitter Followers, and Vocalist to have Performed the Highest Rated and Most-Watched Show in Super Bowl History.

Through her profession, Perry has sold over 100 million records internationally, making her one of the best-selling music specialists ever.

How To Succeed In Life

1. You Will Feel the Pain

Every successful person travels a painful journey. Suffering is an integral and essential part of any real pursuit of success. Nothing about success comes easy, but every painful story has the potential to have a successful ending. You may as well accept suffering as a travelling companion rather than resist it and create more struggle. See each day as a day that you are blessed with new chances and opportunities to start from where you find yourself. Uncertainty and stress are inevitable. Both prompt you to make adjustments to mitigate their effects, mentoring you toward further success. A little stress can push you in a positive direction.

2. You Will Want To Give Up Prematurely

As you wander through your more directionless times on your journey, you will experience intense moments of feeling lost and hopeless. It is during these times you must hold tight to your vision and take back control of your motivation. You must prepare yourself mentally to fight that little voice inside your head that becomes a force to reckon with when you have to push yourself to keep going when you don't feel like it. The quickest way to derail your dreams is to quit when things look bleak. Quitting when you are on the front lines of these critical moments keeps you living amongst the average. The successful persevere and rise.

3. You Will Lose Relationships

As you succeed, a handful of people will not be willing to support you. Success takes a tremendous amount of effort and sacrifice. The effort and time you need to put into your journey will not be tolerable to some who feel you owe them more of your time, effort, or energy. The successful sacrifice an enormous amount to get to where they want to go, trusting that the people meant to travel their journey with them will accept and support the sacrifices that must be made. You will likely lose relationships with those who do not passionately share in your vision. As you succeed, your path will narrow; fewer people are at the top.

4. People Will Discourage You

There is a popular thought that you should keep your dreams close to your chest because if you share them, you may pillage them to dream-stealers and naysayers. The human mind is programmed to believe the negative. Negative thoughts are extremely contagious, and when you set out, you will have an audience full of small-minded people trying to scare you and discourage you from chasing your dreams. These people want to instil so much fear in you that you shrink. You have to make yourself immune to these influences when you set out on your quest for success. Work quietly and let your success do the talking.

5. You Will Be Hated For No Reason

The reality is that people don't tend to like other successful people. There is a jealousy that comes along with being different, standing out, and humbly chasing your dreams. Small people hate those who have or do everything they lack. Dealing with jealousy can be difficult, especially if you want to maintain relationships with certain people or if they are a big part of your life. You may need to let them go. In reality, there will always be a certain percentage of people who will not like you, no matter who you are or what you do. Use these people and experiences as resiliency training and reasons to fuel your drive. Success is always the greatest revenge. Learn to let your haters make you greater.

Exercise For You

Creative Expression Exercise

Experiment with a form of creative expression that you haven't explored before. This could be writing, drawing, singing, or any other artistic endeavor. Share your creation with a friend or online community to gather feedback and encouragement.

Bill Gates – The Team Maker!

"Bringing together the right information with the right people will dramatically improve a company's ability to develop and act on strategic business opportunities."

Bill Gates is a visionary who understands the power of collaboration and the limitations of solitary endeavours. In the modern world, attempting to accomplish great feats single-handedly often hampers progress. While certain tasks can be undertaken individually, others necessitate the collective efforts of a team.

Bill Gates has captivated the global audience through his unwavering dedication to Microsoft. While you may already be familiar with the Microsoft narrative and Bill's role as a co-founder, grasping the back-breaking journey that led to this extraordinary achievement is essential. Motivated to make a meaningful impact on the world, Bill embarked on coding projects in the mid-70s. These endeavours eventually materialized in the establishment of Microsoft in 1975. Today, Microsoft stands tall with a staggering valuation exceeding $2.5

trillion[15]. How did this remarkable entrepreneur navigate the numerous challenges, maintain his focus, and realize his goals? Before we delve into the trials faced by Bill Gates, it is crucial to recognize that regardless of your current position in life, you have undoubtedly made remarkable progress.

The Journey's Trials: Albuquerque

Bill Gates and Paul Allen founded Microsoft in Albuquerque, New Mexico. In 1975, after seeing an article in Popular Electronics about the Altair 8800, an early personal computer, Gates and Allen wrote a version of the BASIC programming language for it. They then contacted the company that made the Altair, Micro Instrumentation and Telemetry Systems (MITS), based in Albuquerque[16].

Gates and Allen moved to Albuquerque to work with MITS, and it was there that they formally founded Microsoft (initially as "Micro-Soft"). They operated in Albuquerque for several years before eventually relocating the company to the Seattle area in Washington state, where both Gates and Allen were originally from. During their time in Albuquerque, Microsoft grew from a small startup to a more established software company, setting the stage for its future growth and dominance in the industry.

At that time, the future outcome of their endeavours remained uncertain, but their unwavering commitment and tireless efforts eventually etched their names in history. How does Albuquerque exemplify the challenges that inspire the world? Albuquerque stands as a testament that, irrespective of your current circumstances or aspirations, when you embark on the path to realizing your goals, you have the potential to achieve worldwide recognition. Each time the name "Albuquerque" is mentioned, let it serve as a resounding reminder that giving up should never be an option!

The Path to the Future

Like numerous individuals, Bill Gates embarked on his educational journey in high school and ultimately found his way to Harvard University(17). While you may be familiar with the broad strokes of his story, have you truly grasped the profound significance of his choices? Indeed, it is a fact that Bill Gates chose to drop out of Harvard, yet we should never underestimate the profound transformative potential concealed within that decision. Bill Gates is not merely a "dropout"; he left Harvard with a purpose-to establish Microsoft. By examining his trajectory, we discover that Bill Gates had a dream and took the necessary steps to turn that dream into an extraordinary fortune. No one should dictate your will or decisions. Nevertheless, evaluating the feasibility of the future plans that await you is essential. Furthermore, it is worth noting that Bill Gates was also a dedicated team player. At Harvard, he crossed paths with Allen, who astutely recognized his immense potential for greatness. Together, they would create a legacy characterized by extraordinary accomplishments.

Bill and Allen shared a common vision and executed a strategic plan. Yet, their aspirations would have remained mere dreams if they had failed to seize the right opportunity. What was this opportunity, you may wonder? During the early 1970s, technology was characterized by scarcity or near absence. However, with the advent of the "announcement of the Altair 8800 minicomputer hobbyist kit," Bill and Allen recognized its potential and took decisive action. In 1974, they bravely confronted the challenges present in the technological landscape by developing software code, which they subsequently sold to computer manufacturers- this pivotal moment paved the way for an exciting and promising future.

The Inspiring Life of Bill Gates

As human beings, we all experience disappointment and the sting of failure after prolonged struggles. If you have ever felt the weight of failure in your own life, take a moment to recall the word "Albuquerque!" Before Bill Gates could establish Microsoft in Albuquerque, he undoubtedly encountered criticism from friends, family, and strangers. Yet, what a remarkable decision he made! What if he had failed? Would he have regretted his choices in the face of such scrutiny?

Now, consider this: your decisions must acknowledge the potential for success and failure. Nevertheless, you should strive to give your best and diligently work towards achieving success. Thus far, you have gained insights into the courageous actions taken by Bill Gates. Even if your plans encounter setbacks, let the extraordinary success story of Bill Gates serve as the driving force behind your unwavering determination. After all, what if you succeed against all odds despite the possibility of failure?

Bill's Future Road: A High-Risk Investment

It is truly remarkable how an unknown individual in Albuquerque during the 1970s, Bill Gates, transformed into a global icon. Bill Gates's net worth currently stands at an impressive $117 billion[18], showcasing his enduring dedication, astute judgment, tireless efforts, devotion to collaboration, and steadfast perseverance.

The road to Bill's future was a high-risk investment. I called it "investment" because he traded his career as a potential lawyer to learn more about "coding." Bill invested in himself. Instead of facing the classroom walls or listening to the professors in college, he dedicated his time to reading, interpreting, and writing codes.

Bill Gates was a decision-making genius. One of the things you must embrace to push yourself further is decision-making. You may give up easily if you can't make the right decision. If they had calculated the risk and failed to see the success, Bill Gates would have given up on his dream. Everything you do involves some level of risk. For example, Bill was given the option of "dropping out of school in order to make a global record" or "staying in college and becoming a future lawyer." There are dangers in either case. Ensure you make the best decision you can and back it up with the best evidence you can find - this will be the power that strengthens your decision and makes you impervious to giving up!

The Inspirational Steps in Bill Gates' Success Story

Passion: The power of passion cannot be underestimated when it comes to sustaining determination and refusing to give up. Since the 8th grade, Bill Gates has demonstrated an unwavering passion for technology and coding. His relentless pursuit of knowledge, dedication to learning, and diligent work ethic are all fueled by his deep-rooted passion. How strong is your passion? Are you prepared to make sacrifices in pursuit of your aspirations? Always remember, never give up!

Decision-Making: Bill Gates faced a critical crossroads where he had to choose between following a conventional career path and pursuing his true passion. He bravely opted to pursue his passion, and today, we are discussing his remarkable story. By staying resolute and refusing to quit, your own choices hold the power to guide you towards happiness and fulfilment.

Hard Work: Bill Gates is renowned for his exceptional work ethic and unwavering dedication. It is not by chance that he left behind a promising career and never became complacent. Regardless of your circumstances, take inspiration from the "magic of history." Visualize individuals like Bill Gates, who assumed multiple roles as a sales manager and programmer in the early days of Microsoft during the 1980s.

Teamwork: The power of teamwork cannot be understated when it comes to combating laziness, inertia, and unproductivity. Bill Gates is an exemplary team player, as demonstrated by his partnership with Allen, a fellow visionary who shared the same passion. Together, they achieved extraordinary success by leveraging their collective strengths.

Persistence: In the nascent days of the technology industry, established companies held a greater allure for investors than new ventures. Bill Gates encountered numerous challenges along his journey, but it was his unwavering persistence that we read and write about today. You, too, can cultivate persistence within yourself. Never give up, for your persistence can pave the way to remarkable achievements.[19]

Exercises For You

Networking and Collaboration Challenge

Identify one area in your life or career where collaboration and networking can play a crucial role. Actively seek out opportunities to connect with others, share ideas, and collaborate on a project. Use Bill Gates' emphasis on collaboration as a model for achieving success through teamwork.

Hard Work and Dedication Action Plan

Develop a plan to enhance your work ethic and dedication to your goals. Identify specific actions you can take to work more efficiently and consistently towards your aspirations. Use Bill Gates' commitment to hard work as motivation for your own efforts.

Bethany Hamilton: The one-armed professional Surfer

"Courage doesn't mean you don't get afraid. Courage means you don't let the fear stop you."

When we hear the name Bill Gates, most of us can easily recall facts about his life. However, Bethany Hamilton's remarkable journey will touch your heart and change your perspective on life. Showcasing unwavering determination in the face of adversity, her story serves as an inspiration to millions worldwide. Bethany Hamilton is the true definition of determination. How determined are you to achieve your goals, even if you lose one of your arms trying?

Bethany Hamilton's story will break and melt your heart with powerful, inspiring determination to strike harder and NEVER GIVE UP!

About Bethany Hamilton

Bethany Hamilton has earned over 20 prestigious awards, each a testament to her exceptional talent and unwavering spirit. She holds the title of "comeback athlete" in various esteemed competitions, including those organized by Nickelodeon, FOX Teen, the United States Sports Academy, and ESPY[20]. Having been born and raised in Hawaii, her profound bond with the water began from a young age. At a mere 8 years old, she embarked on her surfing expedition, fueled by the aspiration of becoming a popular surfer, until her life took an unexpected turn.

Hamilton has several honours and awards in surfing; she's a figure of courage and determination to athletes globally. How did a small girl in Hawaii make global history?

At 13, Bethany Hamilton faced a defining moment that would shape her future and inspire athletes worldwide. Engaging in a surfing session alongside her best friend, her best friend's father, and her brothers, she fell victim to a tiger shark attack, resulting in the tragic loss of her arm. Many would have viewed this incident as an insurmountable setback, leading to a drastic change in career paths. However, at the tender age of 13, Bethany Hamilton refused to succumb to despair, making her story truly awe-inspiring. Despite the harrowing encounter with the tiger shark, she resolved to persevere[21].

What an inspiring story! She refused to give up even after a tiger shark attack that cost her arm. Bethany fearlessly returned to the water, pursuing her passion for surfing with unwavering determination. With her extraordinary resilience, she introduced herself to the world and astounded everyone by surpassing all expectations with her remarkable abilities.

Bethany Hamilton's Indomitable Spirit

Hamilton's achievements in the world of surfing have garnered numerous accolades, demonstrating her immense impact as an athlete. She proved her name "Hamilton" as a special keyword to computers, humans, and sports. If you type her name on your computer, you will see many stories about her, telling how she proved her point. *But, what point?* Also, if you ask several people, "Who is Bethany Hamilton?" many of them reply as "The athlete that survived a tiger shark attack." Yes, she proved her point. *But, what point?* Lastly, Hamilton is an icon in the history of the sport. She also proved her point. *But, what point?*

Hamilton tells you never to give up. Her point and message to you are that "You should believe in yourself." She delivers her points, saying, *"If you cannot fly, you should run. If you cannot run, you should walk; you should crawl if you cannot walk."* Her life is pictorial evidence of this quote by Martin Luther King Jr. Hamilton laid on her water board with two hands, paddling and aiming for the surfing championship. However, the circumstances of life reduced the arm to one, but she never gave up!

Bethany Hamilton's Personal Life

Her journey stands as a poignant testament, emphasizing the unwavering truth that, Bethany Hamilton's personal life is extraordinary in its own right. Yes, her courageous action gave her the love of her life, who appreciated and loved her like that. Despite experiencing the unfortunate loss of her arm and encountering early career challenges, she has successfully forged a path toward love, marital bliss, and parenthood.

Hamilton's personal life keeps telling you that irrespective of our journeys, there exist individuals within our global community who wholeheartedly embrace and appreciate our intrinsic worth and uniqueness. By never abandoning her dreams, even in the face of setbacks, Bethany Hamilton has inspired all.

Everyone faces setbacks in life. What may seem like a setback could actually be a launching pad for greater achievements. If Hamilton had her arms intact, she might not have pushed herself to train harder or set loftier goals. Yet, observing her dedication and resilience, one can't help but wonder about the intensity of her training to compete against athletes without any physical limitations.

Key Lessons from Bethany Hamilton's Experiences

1. **Life Is Unpredictable:** Life's unpredictability and the uncontrollable forces of nature emphasize the need to make the most out of our circumstances. Some are born into privilege, while others must

work tirelessly to achieve greatness. Some face early adversity, while others lead short lives. Bethany Hamilton teaches us to transform the unpredictable into the predictable by refusing to give up.

She suffered the loss of an arm (an unpredictable circumstance) but made it to the world championship because she did not give up.

2. **Nothing Is Unfair:** Life is not inherently unfair. We should refrain from perceiving success as evidence of life's injustices. Regardless of our current circumstances, our present actions hold power to shape the future and define our position in history. Everyone faces challenges, but we can create our own sense of fairness by persevering and never giving up.

3. **She Knew What She Wanted:** Hamilton spent her whole life trying to achieve her goal. Instead of succumbing to despair, she spent her life rebuilding what seemed lost. This extraordinary approach serves as a powerful reminder that each of us possesses the strength to do the same.

5 Ways to Make Your Dreams Come True

1. Strip Your Goals and Narrow Them to the End

Ensure you handle your dreams perfectly and do this by stripping them to the last thing you can think of. For example, having more goals at a time demands more from you. If you can reduce the goals to one at a time, you will have the best route by which you can earn your value.

2. Do Not Give In to Fear

Another crucial tip is to face your fear head-on. Ensure that you are not a target for fear. It's natural for people to feel fear whenever they decide to move upward. If it is because you are leaving your comfort zone, it is natural and normal. Your body's physical makeup may cause you to feel uneasy about the new changes, which can lead to fear. When pursuing your dream, be sure to always be prepared. Make sure you overcome any fears that may arise.

3. **Be Committed and Act Now**

It is easy to turn back if you are not committed. You may never progress if all you do is wish for better things. Our worth is not determined by our ability to succeed but rather by the things we have accomplished. It would be best to live a life that adds value to you, makes you act at the appropriate time, and gives you better options to succeed in life. What if you are meant to do great, but the inability to differentiate "wishing time" and "action time" delays you?

4. **Suck and Grab Ideas from Anyone and Anywhere**

Most likely, someone has already done what you want to do. If you are not too proud to admit it, you can always learn from what others have done. You can always learn from other people's books and contributions to life. There are many books, videos, and lectures from experts that can help you reach your next goal or dream. This book is one of them. Sometimes, you might need a mentor to help you along the way. A mentor doesn't have to be there in person.

5. **Be Vigilant and Consistent**

If you want to succeed, stay focused on your goals. Remind yourself why you started the journey in the first place. Allow it to come to you naturally. Keep some values or items around you that remind you of your dream. For example, if you want to be an NBA superstar, you can surround yourself with images of great NBA players-on your phone, in your closet, and so on. All of these would serve as reminders of who you are and what you must accomplish in the end.

Exercises For You

Create a Vision Board

Bethany Hamilton's story is about resilience and vision. Create a vision board that represents your goals and dreams. Include images, quotes, and symbols that inspire you. Place the vision board where you can see it daily.

Practice Daily Affirmations

Bethany's indomitable spirit is fueled by her positive mindset. Incorporate daily affirmations into your routine. Create affirmations that resonate with your goals and repeat them daily to reinforce a positive mindset.

Jim Carrey: Story Of Endurance

"Life opens up opportunities to you, and you either take them or you stay afraid of taking them."

Jim Carrey is acclaimed for his unforgettable roles in movies and television, but his character goes beyond his on-screen talent. He has cultivated an amazing sense of humour and impressive communication abilities, even though he struggles with dyslexia. Despite his learning disorder, his talent and perseverance make his success even more noteworthy. How did Jim Carrey, despite his dyslexia, become a globally renowned actor and comedian?

Endurance has been the key to all of Jim's accomplishments. He endured the difficulties he faced in school and remained resilient in his pursuit of greatness. Jim followed his passion relentlessly, and today, we are inspired by his story, which teaches us never to give up.

Early Life of Jim Carrey

Dyslexia, a condition that makes learning and acquiring new skills challenging, was not unfamiliar to Jim from a young age[22]. During his educational journey, Jim encountered censure not only from his schoolmates but also from his tutors. One of his teachers labelled him as "brilliant but disruptive" due to his tendency to disturb the class after completing his assignments. While such comments may seem commonplace, it is important to note that the teacher specifically pointed out Jim's condition. Imagine being a child and being singled out in such a manner.

Despite facing considerable criticism, Jim managed to stay happy and inspiring. He would mimic actions in front of mirrors, honing his ability to empathize and connect with others through free expression. Jim adopted various approaches to bridge the gap caused by his dyslexia, never allowing himself to be intimidated. He convinced himself to envision a better version of who he could become.

Jim started creating funny acts to make people laugh, make friends, and experience the joy of communication. Naturally, with dyslexia, it wasn't easy for Jim to approach a random person and say "Hi." Instead, he wrote letters to movie industries, showcasing his talent for humorous acts and other skills he had to offer.

No Money but Vision

Jim's family did not have financial abundance. Money was yet another obstacle he had to overcome. They lived in an unfavourable neighbourhood with low-rent apartments. Although Jim's story is worth reading, his experiences were far from desirable. He faced the challenge of not having enough funds but possessed a strong vision to create a path that would bring prosperity to his family. At 16, Jim made a decision that greatly impacted his future. Like Bill Gates, decision-making proved his greatest asset in difficult circumstances.

In the 10th grade, he attempted to juggle eight-hour night shifts at work with attending school during the day. Exhausted to the point of not comprehending what his teachers were teaching, Jim found himself isolated at school, fearing that anyone who approached him would discover his embarrassing neediness. At this point, Jim prioritized his privacy over making new friends.

He felt that school was wasting his time, offering little learning and meaningful connections. Consequently, displaying immense courage, he opted to drop out of the educational system at 16. What came next? Due to the challenges of dealing with life, family, and personal needs simultaneously, he made a spontaneous decision.

Realizing that their environment and current circumstances were leading them astray, Jim's family gathered together and moved to Canada despite having no job prospects or a promising future. His parents and siblings lived in a van for eight months, travelling between campgrounds, never settling in one place for long.

One can only imagine Jim's mental burden during this time-the frustration of losing out on his high school years, feeling intellectually behind, the humiliation, and the struggles of poverty. However, perhaps that sense of mediocrity prepared him for future success, instilling in him a determination to exert more effort than others.

Effort Defies Measurement

Our efforts cannot be quantified, and even if we fail, people may not notice. No matter how hard the road ahead is, never stop striving towards your goal. Bill Gates' story may have faded into obscurity if he had remained at Harvard, and Hamilton would not inspire us today if she had given up on her dreams. You may never get the chance to share your own story if you give up today.

Who knows the future? No one! Right. However, you can shape your future and direct it towards success. Today can be the foundation for a better tomorrow.

Jim Carrey Today

Despite his struggles, Jim Carrey has become a prominent figure today. He graces the pages of numerous magazines, and his accomplishments are documented in various books. Considered by numerous individuals as one of the best comedians in history, his remarkable presence in the film industry is unforgettable. Some of his notable contributions to the movie industry include;

- The Truman Show
- Eternal Sunshine of the Spotless Mind
- Dumb and Dumber To
- Ace Ventura: Pet Detective
- The Mask
- Man on the Moon
- Kick-Ass 2

With over 45 awards and numerous nominations, Jim Carrey has been renowned for his powerful and varied performances. His masterful role in "Man on the Moon" in 2000 was honoured with a Golden Globe. He was awarded for starring roles in smash hits such as:

- How the Grinch Stole Christmas (2001)
- Dumb & Dumber (1995).

As a result, he was bestowed with the MTV Movie & TV Award and Kids' Choice Award for Favorite Movie Actor in 1995, 2001, and 2004[23].

The Summary of Jim Carrey's Life

As Jim often mentions in his interviews, he is a true champion who never gives up. His life is a powerful lesson on overcoming barriers in the journey towards greatness. With his motivational words ringing in our ears, we can trust that there are limitless opportunities for people to accomplish great feats, provided that they remain undeterred. Today is meant for building tomorrow. But what if the present feels overwhelming? What if hardships seem insurmountable? What if the journey becomes unbearably difficult?

In those moments, you can find solace and guidance by reading about role models like Jim Carrey. Jim is an exemplary figure for those with dyslexia, and even without explicitly sharing his experiences, his life speaks volumes about the importance of perseverance.

Bill Gates' life is an example of a great negotiator and a visionary. Each of their lives highlights the significance of not giving up on your dreams. Although the path may not always be illuminated, just like it wasn't for Bill at Harvard or Jim in the 1970s in Canada, they both made it, and we bear witness to their incredible success.

By reading about the lives of those you aspire to emulate, such as Jim Carrey, this book can help keep you on track. If you aspire to succeed, be like Jim Carrey-NEVER GIVE UP!

Life-Changing Lessons from Jim Carrey

1. **Jim Shows You Are The Light Of The World:** No matter how you think in the darkness, if you work uprightly on the right path, you will shine, and people shall behold you. Everyone is equal in the world; however, our efforts and perspectives make us different. Some kids born to rich and noble families may decide to enjoy a life regarded

as "slum." Whatever you do, remember you are telling people what they should say, see, and write about you.

2. **You Are Not Life's Object; You Are The Subject:** Life doesn't happen to you. Anything that occurs in your life happens for you. Yes! For your greatness, success and story. No matter the story or how Jim's bio is written, his life will always be in the form of "before and after" his success. Whatever is named "before" is the thing that prepares you for the "after." However, this may not be pleasant. Still, never give up.

3. **Take A Chance To Do What You Love Instead Of Giving Up:** Jim might have given up when his colleagues preyed on him, teachers spoke badly about him, or the neediness rekindled after he left school and more life challenges emerged. No! He instead pursues what he loves most and makes a fortune.

4. **Today Is Not The Limitation Of Tomorrow:** Your present situation is not permanent. Thus, it cannot determine tomorrow. You could become whomever you want if you strike harder, remain persistent, and work hard.

5. **Stop Being Sensitive:** If you must do great, you should focus on yourself, avoid being sensitive to people's reactions and be good to yourself. If you hate yourself, it would be hard to keep going. Whatever happens now, make sure you love the

person you are and strike harder today and tomorrow until you have it all.

Exercises For You

Overcome Criticism with Self-Love

Jim Carrey faced criticism throughout his life, but he embraced self-love. Identify an area in your life where you've faced criticism or negative feedback. Develop strategies to overcome self-doubt and cultivate self-love in the face of external opinions.

Engage in Random Acts of Kindness

Jim's message includes the importance of being good to yourself and others. Engage in random acts of kindness in your daily life. This could be as simple as offering a kind word, helping someone in need, or expressing gratitude. Record your acts of kindness and reflect on the positive impact they have on you and others.

Be like Jim; Never Give Up!

Walt Disney: Tasted Failure But Didn't Give Up

"It is good to have a failure while you're young because it teaches you so much, and once you've lived through the worst, you're never quite as vulnerable afterwards."

Walt Disney firmly believed in the adage, "A winner never quits, and a quitter never wins." For Disney, this phrase encapsulated a lifetime of experiences. He was born into a challenging situation, lived through it, and emerged victorious. His achievements resonate even today, as his impact has touched people worldwide in various ways. He revolutionized the visual and audio industry so much that his contributions are omnipresent. However, the story behind his success is an inspiring tale with valuable lessons.

Embracing Self-Improvement and Nurturing Imagination

Have you ever worked tirelessly, only to find yourself unable to fulfil your basic needs despite receiving payment? It's unlikely. Disney faced the arduous task of working long hours, only to have his father seize all the earnings and return to his comfortable lifestyle, leaving Disney's needs unattended. The creator and voice of Mickey Mouse started his journey from home, where he encountered numerous struggles. For a short period, Disney had to sell newspapers and snacks on the train daily to meet the basic requirements of his family[24]. Unfortunately, their father played a major role in their hardships. At a young age, Disney's brother left home, unable to bear the difficulties any longer. The situation seemed bleak, but Disney refused to give up on his talent.

Disney could have settled for a job at a local store and abandoned his dreams. However, he chose to volunteer, dedicating himself to learning and honing his drawing skills. Disney modestly embarked on his animation career. He began creating drawings from his imagination and sold them to relatives and neighbours for a small fee. Little did he know that these seemingly insignificant efforts would yield tremendous rewards in the future.

Overcoming Adversity Through Perseverance and Dedication

Rather than succumbing to adversity, Disney focused on self-improvement. He acknowledged the greatness within him and sought to nurture his talent by exploring the realms of painting and drawing. He enrolled in drawing and photography classes, demonstrating his determination amidst hardship and adversity. Nelson Mandela once said that education is a powerful instrument for changing the world[25], and Disney not only changed the world but also transformed himself. Imagination lays the foundation for innovation, and Disney combined the two, nurturing his imagination so that his innovative ideas could come to fruition.

Disney persevered in his pursuit of learning, even when faced with anxiety, excuses, and frustration. If one lacks the right mindset, these challenges can easily lead to giving up. Although Disney was not exposed to the importance of education early on, he knew what he wanted. He recognized that enduring temporary suffering through learning was necessary to avoid prolonged hardship in the future. Strategic thinking, adaptability, and unwavering dedication to oneself and one's dreams are crucial factors in overcoming obstacles.

Failure as a Catalyst for Growth and Reinvention

Many circumstances could have pushed Disney to the brink of giving up, directly or indirectly. For instance, learning amidst hardship may seem almost impossible.

However, Disney understood that to achieve greatness, he needed to master the art of drawing and painting. The challenges of gathering funds for his classes were daunting, but his unwavering determination paved the way for opportunities.

Yes! There were more opportunities but even more failures!

At 19, in Kansas City, Disney embarked on pursuing his long-standing dream: establishing his own company in 1920. Despite limited resources, he still chose to launch his first animation project. Relying on the support of friends, he began with small steps, only to realize a heartbreaking failure in the end. Despite the monumental nature of his endeavour, his attempts to monetize his animations did not pan out. Yet, he did not let failure deter him. In fact, failure became the catalyst that propelled him forward. How can one thrive in the face of failure? Did you cease to try after failing the first time? If you did, it's time to muster the strength to try even harder. A first-time failure does not equate to abandoning the dreams that resonate within you. The journey continues; it's just a matter of strategizing and reevaluating your approach.

The Pursuit of Dreams Amidst Setbacks and Disappointments

He tried harder, again, with another strategy! But...

The interesting part of Disney's story is that "he tried harder even after his failure from the first attempt."

Following his bankruptcy, he pursued employment as a visual artist in a newspaper. However, his contract was terminated shortly after he started, with the manager citing his lack of passion, creativity, and imagination[26]. It seemed that Disney had failed both as an entrepreneur and an employee. Few individuals find themselves in such a position of facing failure in both roles. Nevertheless, Disney never relinquished his dreams.

Driven by his childhood aspirations, Disney left Kansas City for Hollywood, leaving behind his previous experiences in search of new and promising opportunities. His decision exemplified strategic thinking. He established an animation studio in Hollywood and toiled for five years without pay, profit, or income. Finally, after a long wait, Disney succeeded with the release of the short films "Alice in Cartoonland" and "Oswald the Lucky Rabbit" in 1927. This could have been the beginning of a prosperous business venture. However, he lost the copyright to his characters in the same year, facing yet another setback[27]. The closer Disney got to his dreams, the more challenges he encountered. Yet, HE NEVER GAVE UP!

Success Amidst Hardship: Mickey Mouse and the Turning Point

The path to victory was within reach, yet another phase of hardship awaited Disney. This time, he succeeded in crafting a character but could not capture his viewers' attention. Similarly, his attempts with another character were met with rejection from distributors.

It wasn't until 1934 that Disney faced multiple failures. He established his company in 1920 but had to endure until 1934 for his efforts to bear fruit. What transpired during that period? A lengthy 14 years. Walt Disney underwent significant personal growth, navigating the early hardships and subsequent failures, starting from 19. Once he reached 34, he found his aspirations coming true.

Taking Risks and Transforming Dreams into Reality

Finally, on his third attempt, Disney achieved success. Mickey Mouse became a sensation, marking a turning point in his career. Disney had yearned for this breakthrough and transformed his dreams into reality. Despite widespread scepticism in 1934, he aspired to create a full-length animated film. After three years and high production costs, Disney was under financial duress, having to place his home up for a mortgage and in danger of being homeless. However, to Disney, the risk was worth it. The resulting film became the highlight of 1938, setting the stage for immense success in the industry. After producing the celebrated Pluto Cartoon series and the timeless characters of Donald Duck, Mickey Mouse, and Goofy, Disney continued to develop an abundance of iconic figures. Ultimately, he established Walt Disney Studios and, in 1955, opened Disneyland Theme Park[28], which became renowned worldwide.

Walt Disney's Net Worth and Awards

The value of Disney's ownership in the Disney Creation company alone was $600 million. He also claimed the largest individual stake in Walt Disney Inc. When he passed away, he left 45% of his wealth for his wife and children, and another 45% went to charity. The remaining share of his wealth went to his sister, nieces, and nephews and 45% of his house to his better half and children as a family trust[29].

At the time of his passing, the value of Disney's various assets ranged from $100 to $150 million, or $750 million to $1.1 billion today[29].

5 Ways Not to Give Up on Your Dream

1. Embrace A Mindset Of Perseverance, Never Giving Up

People often surrender when faced with unexpected setbacks while pursuing their tasks. But what if the project you envisioned, which seemed so promising, fails to materialize? In such moments, it becomes crucial to reassess our plans. It is essential to grasp the underlying principle of plans-they should not be rigid. While your ultimate goal remains constant, numerous paths exist to achieve it. On your journey towards personal success, if one approach fails to yield results, strive to develop another. Always remember that your commitment to overcoming challenges is a testament to never giving up on your aspirations.

2. Watch A Persevering Individual

Observe a determined individual, whether through a movie or alternative methods. The key is to connect with someone who has experienced the same challenges you are currently facing. How does their journey resonate with you? What emotions and memories does it evoke? Engage deeply with the movie or story, as it will prepare your mind for future tasks. By immersing yourself in the perseverance of another person today, you equip yourself for the challenges of tomorrow. For instance, Sylvester Stallone witnessed Muhammad Ali's match and drew the inspiration that transformed his life. This exemplifies the significance of such experiences. Some life experiences are embedded in those movies, and if you overlook these cinematic treasures, you miss out on valuable lessons that can guide you throughout your journey.

3. Reflect On "Why" You Started

Reflect on the "Why" behind your initial motivation. Why did you embark on this journey? What convinced you that you could succeed? And what drove you to come this far? Revisiting the past is a means to forge a connection with the future. Remember, while your current circumstances are significant, the ultimate outcome lies in the present and the past. If feasible, embark on a "journey to the past." Delve into your personal history and examine the fundamentals. This exploration will enable you to avoid repeating past mistakes and propel your life forward. Whenever you find yourself pondering, "Why am I here?" it signifies a desire to understand the genesis of your journey from your present standpoint. You can unlearn past errors and embrace more effective approaches by rewinding the timeline.

4. Call Or Talk To Someone

Beyonce found solace in her father, someone she could confide in. He not only became her manager but also took thorough care of her career. This indicates that he understood what needed to be done and how to accomplish it effectively. The key is to have someone you can talk to who truly comprehends you and knows the necessary steps to take. It's essential to establish the best communication channel that works for you. The person you confide in should be genuinely invested in your progress. When you share your challenges with them, they will do their utmost to support your growth and well-being. So, when you're feeling down, who do you think you can call upon for this kind of support?

5. Failures Should Be A Stepping Stone

Failures should serve as stepping stones on your journey. The key lies in seeking the best approach to leverage your present or past failures and turn them into opportunities for growth. Underestimating the power of failure would be a mistake. Just because you fail today does not mean the same fate awaits you tomorrow, especially if you wholeheartedly invest your efforts. A case in point is Hillary Clinton, who, in 2008, as the junior United States Senator from New York, aspired to become the nation's leader. Despite campaigning vigorously, she did not secure the Democratic faction's nomination. However, she refused to abandon her goal.

Instead, she accepted the position of Secretary of State, a move that brought her one step closer to the White House. It served as a stepping stone for her ambitions.

Exercise For You

Adapt and Reinvent

Consider a goal or project that hasn't yielded the expected results. Explore alternative approaches to achieve the same goal. Embrace the idea of adapting and reinventing your strategies, just as Disney did throughout his journey.

J.K. Rowling – All About Her Inspiring World

"It is impossible to live without failing at something unless you live so cautiously that you might as well not have lived at all – in which case, you fail by default."

J.K. Rowling achieved the first billionaire author status[30], but her path to success was filled with inspiring stories worth exploring before you contemplate giving up on your goals. Rowling is a conqueror; she overcame several hurdles along her journey. For instance, she wrote her beloved Harry Potter story while travelling on a train. This highlights the importance of recognizing the right opportunities and knowing when to seize them. Instead of postponing until she made it to her destination, Rowling captured the tale while it was still fresh in her mind.

It's crucial not to close yourself to opportunities just because you face challenges. If you're engaged in creative pursuits or envisioning a particular way of life, it's essential to let your subconscious mind communicate with you regularly. Why is this significant? Our subconscious mind actively seeks solutions, especially when we are facing difficulties. For example, you might suddenly recall the names of your debtors when you're short on cash. If this has ever happened to you, it's worth pondering why you remembered them precisely when you needed money.

You never know where the ideas swirling in your mind might lead you. The power to determine the level of acceptance your new ideas will receive lies beyond your control. For example, a movie can garner millions of views overnight, while the actor behind it may struggle financially. Until you start executing your ideas, you can neither agree nor disagree with yourself. Rowling herself became a philanthropist, screenwriter, and producer-all thanks to a single story, Harry Potter. The idea you keep postponing might be the one that eventually propels you into the world. Harry Potter, the tale of dark wizards and saviours, became a best-selling book.

Endurance, Creativity, and Perseverance

At the point of writing Harry Potter, J.K. Rowling faced numerous struggles both in her own life and beyond. It took her 7 years to compile and produce the first book in the series[31]. While facing all the hardships, she exhibited incredible resilience and determination.

One thing that works during hardship is to nurture and elevate your creativity instead of giving up. As I said earlier, your soul, body, and spirit are ready to furnish your ideas with a final product, especially during times of trouble. However, we always give room to fear and anxiety, which eat up the ideas. Generally, sad and happy poems resonate more deeply because human emotions operate on different levels when we experience sadness or joy. Whenever you find yourself in an unconventional state of mind, harness that moment to fuel your creative endeavours.

Rowling embraced her life's challenges and realized that anxiety and complaints wouldn't solve her problems. Instead, she needed to find a solution and did find the solution on a train ride. Even though she built the road that led to her success, it took her 7 years to finish the work she started. How long can you wait to see the fruits of your labour? Do you give up on the way to success? The response should be a decisive no.

We cannot write our success stories overnight; we must work for them, sweat them, and take responsibility. Unless you want to deceive yourself, waiting for the victory ahead without any effort is unrealistic. Rowling did not only wait; she improved herself to welcome the great things ahead of her. Despite achieving fame and prominence as a published author, she likewise ventured into producing and scripting for film and television.

Have you considered yourself a failure when you haven't reached your desired position? You shouldn't. Rowling didn't rush her progress or skip any learning experiences. She diligently studied, patiently waited, and obediently absorbed knowledge. It's important to give your ideas the respect they deserve before they can flourish. Many people out there admire and desire your talents and capabilities, yet they have nothing to offer in return.

However, you possess a wealth of ideas flowing through your mind. If you fail to wait and bring your ideas to fruition, you may experience regret, especially when you see others who patiently wait. Waiting for the right timing is normal, and it's okay to encounter failures along the way. There's no set timeframe for success-you might achieve it at a young age or later in life.

Personal Struggles and Life Circumstances Causing Delays

During the inception of her content, Rowling encountered several issues, which led to the postponement of her story. Unconsciously, her vision was put on hold. She could have ultimately given up and pursued a different path in life. Ironically, a minor setback caused her story to be delayed for seven years. In 1991, she relocated to Portugal to teach, where she met Jorge Arantes and married him[32]. The couple had a daughter, but Rowling soon filed for divorce. Being jobless, separated, and a single parent left her devastated. She was diagnosed with clinical depression, battling divorce, raising a child alone, and navigating life-threatening challenges. All these factors contributed to the delayed emergence of her story seven years after its conception.

Harry Potter's Story Faces Rejection

In 1995, Rowling completed her first book's manuscript but lacked the funds to publish it. Undeterred, she approached around twelve major publishing companies, all of whom rejected the Harry Potter script. However, she persisted and continued approaching other publishers. Finally, a small publishing company agreed to release 500 copies of Harry Potter, and her perseverance paid off[33]. The book progressed into a set of seven publications, issued from 1997 to 2007. Eventually, the book won numerous notable honours, including the British Book Award and the Nestle Smarties Book Prize for the Year's Children's Book[34]. By 2018, 500 million editions of Harry Potter had been traded around the globe, translated into 80 languages[35]. The book was also adapted into a successful film series, generating billions in revenue.

Exercises For You

Capture Ideas in Unexpected Moments

Pay attention to your thoughts and ideas during unconventional moments, just as J. K. Rowling did while traveling on a train. Keep a small notebook or use a note-taking app to capture ideas that come to you unexpectedly. Review these ideas regularly and consider developing them further.

Avoid Closing Yourself to Opportunities

Evaluate your current mindset and openness to opportunities. Identify any biases or limitations you may have placed on yourself. Commit to being more open to unexpected opportunities and explore areas outside your comfort zone.

Execute Your Ideas

Select one idea that you've been postponing and commit to executing it. Develop a plan of action and set achievable milestones. Take the first step toward bringing this idea to fruition, and acknowledge the power of execution in turning concepts into reality.

Stephen King – The Perseverance Hero

"Remember, hope is a good thing, maybe the best of things, and no good thing ever dies."

Stephen King is a great person who is considered a hero by many people, including his mom, wife, and children. He is a go-getter who never gives up. He talks less and lets his achievements speak for themselves. If you are going through something challenging right now and are about to give up, the story of Stephen King will inspire you to keep pushing. So, ensure you read this chapter until the end. Stephen King, in my own opinion, is one of the greatest heroes of our lifetime. He is hardworking, disciplined, resilient, and focused and deserves all his achievements.

Personal Life and Endurance

Stephen King was born on September 21, 1947, in Portland, Maine, to his lovely parents, Donald and Ruth King. He has a younger sibling known as David. Their parents separated, and the two siblings were raised by their mom. His mom was not financially stable, but luckily, she got financial support from other relatives. Steven graduated from Lisbon Falls High School in 1996 and later went to the University of Maine, Orono. While at the University, he worked as an Understudy in the Fogler Library. This is also the place where he met his lovely partner, Tabitha[36].

Their solid union was the foundation of King's success in his career. There is no doubt that Stephen was already a good writer. However, his partner Tabitha played a vital role in taking his writing skills and career in general to another level. For instance, Tabitha was the one who recovered the draft pages of the popular book "Carrie" in the garbage bin that King had thrown because he thought it would never be successful. She not only recovered the draft pages but also encouraged him to continue writing. Without his wife, Mr. King's first novel, Carrie, would never have been retrieved from the dustbin. She also didn't allow King to take on more work because they slowed his creativity and ability to write more stories[36].

The short story above about King's life shows his endurance. His success did not come on a silver platter. In fact, at some point in his life, everything seemed not to be working, so he almost gave up on writing. He struggled a lot, yet he did not give up. This is the type of fighting spirit you need to develop if you would want to succeed in this world. Whether you are struggling emotionally, financially, or psychologically, don't give up. Keep fighting because that is what it takes to become successful. Also, not every problem can be solved by money. King, in this case, did not have financial problems; he had emotional and psychological issues that barred him from achieving his dreams. However, everything fell into place the moment he developed a positive and stable mindset.

Mr. King had all the reasons to give up on his life, from constant failures in school to a lack of support from his father. In fact, King revealed during an interview that he was not excited to meet his father because he did not support him when he needed it the most. A child needs both parents. A male figure is particularly important for a boy child, and that is what King missed. His dad left when he was about 2 years old and never came back.

Besides lacking a father figure, King was also involved in a grisly accident that nearly took his life. The accident left him with a huge mark on his head. His ribs, lungs, and bones were also damaged. His injuries were so severe that he had to be referred to another hospital for specialised treatment. He had many financial, emotional, and health challenges that almost made him give up. However, all the pain he suffered helped to shape his future[37].

Achievement

Stephen King is, without a doubt, one of the most influential authors in our lifetime. He has dominated the scenes for over 40 years, and his legacy will indeed last forever. King is the first author in history to have over 30 books ranked number 1. To date, King has written more than 70 books, most of which have become social symbols[38].

One of the reasons King became a successful author is because he focused on the right genre. If you have read any of King's books, then you definitely know that he focuses on the horror genre.

How do you identify your strengths? Do you have a preference? Do you have a target? And how do you plan to improve yourself?

If you want to succeed in life, you need to know your strengths, preferences, targets, and how to improve yourself. You can only improve and become better if you constantly work on yourself. You cannot move to the next level if you don't try. Always strive to be better each day. Your yesterday should not determine your today and your future. Regardless of how much you achieve today, you should always strive to get more.

6 Ways to Be Successful in Life

1. Get Yourself Motivated By Staying Committed To Your Goals

You'll find the most motivation when you're truly dedicated to something. Create a reminder system to remember your past efforts, which will help you stay on track every day. It's easy to forget the hard work you've put in if you start slacking off. To achieve the best results, make rules that prioritise motivation over losing motivation. Anyone can get motivated to enjoy life, but not everyone can stay motivated to achieve their goals. Why? Because many people don't know how to keep themselves motivated. So, before you move forward and aim for success, first, find a way to motivate yourself.

2. Learn From The Process

Learn from every step you take towards success, not just the big wins. Pay attention to the small progress you make along the way. Whether things go well or not, there's always something to learn. Successful people don't ignore the journey to success; they make it a habit to appreciate small victories. This will keep you focused and turn your path to your goal into a daily adventure. Along the way, you'll discover interesting things that can help you succeed even more.

3. Think Positively

To have a positive attitude, you should believe in yourself and your ability to succeed. It's important to replace negative thoughts with positive ones to keep yourself motivated even when facing challenges. Think about when babies are learning to walk. They don't give up when they fall. They get back up and keep trying until they can walk and run easily one day. To be successful, you should be open to learning new things and thinking differently than before. Your goals won't happen overnight; they will require practice and effort.

4. Change Your Perspective

To make bad situations better, try changing how you see them. For instance, if you have a terrible day, try to think of it as a good day. This way, you can shift your focus away from the bad stuff. If you can control your thoughts, you'll be more successful. Being able to control things that seem uncontrollable is a valuable skill for success. When you face a tough situation, do you dwell on the problems or give up immediately? If you want to succeed, you should change your attitude. Give yourself a chance to think positively and see how it affects your day or week. If you keep doing this over time, it could lead to success.

5. Keep Trying

What if your current plans don't work out? Don't worry, just try again. And if your next projects also fail, don't give up-try again, too. Keep trying no matter what! It's a good idea to have a schedule when you're working towards your goals. This way, you always know what to do next. Challenge yourself based on your schedule, like saying, "I'll write a better script and send it to different clients by the end of the month," or "I'll save $5,000 by the end of the year." Even if you don't reach your goal, you'll still have progressed from where you started on your schedule. If you plan and keep track of your goals, you'll always have proof that you're improving. Think of it like the Olympics. Not everyone can win medals at the same time, but just participating in the games is a step towards achieving more in life. So, the fact that you're trying now proves that you'll keep trying, even if things get tougher.

6. Don't Exhaust Yourself

It's important to stay enthusiastic about your goal but not tire yourself out. Keeping your journey simple and not working too hard can prevent you from getting tired. Constantly thinking about your goal can wear you out, making something enjoyable feel like a rushed chore. Instead, focus on how much you can learn and achieve over time to avoid getting tired. Manage your time wisely, track your progress, and be open to making changes if your plans aren't working. But don't push yourself too hard.

Exercise For You

Avoid Exhaustion and Prioritize Self-Care

Identify areas of your life where you may be overexerting yourself. Implement self-care practices, such as setting boundaries, taking breaks, or engaging in activities that bring you joy.

Oprah Winfrey – Suffered but Thrived at Last

"Challenges are gifts that force us to search for a new center of gravity. Don't fight them. Just find a new way to stand."

Oprah Winfrey's journey began in challenging circumstances, as she was born to a young, single mother, exposing her to hardships from an early age. From a young age, she encountered sexual abuse, emotional stress, and even PTSD. Despite facing adversity that most children her age couldn't comprehend, Oprah persevered and emerged as an inspirational figure.

Early Challenges and Discovering Strength

Oprah Winfrey was born on January 29, 1954, to a young single mother in Mississippi. Vernita Lee, her mom, had only recently reached 18 when she found herself struggling to provide for her newborn child. Oprah's father, Vernon Winfrey, left the family shortly after her birth, leaving them to face the challenges of life without him[39].

With little means to support Oprah, Vernita made the heart-wrenching decision to leave her daughter in the care of Oprah's maternal grandmother, Hattie Mae Lee. Oprah's early years were marked by separation from her mother and exposure to poverty and hardship. While kids her age were playing and enjoying their childhood, Oprah had to grapple with emotional stress and trauma well beyond her years[40].

Living with her grandmother proved to be a turning point in Oprah's life. Unable to afford many toys or luxuries, Oprah found solace in books. Even as a youngster, she had an immense appetite for perusing and threw herself into the realm of books. Despite not attending kindergarten, Oprah's curiosity and thirst for knowledge led her to teach herself many things. Books became her sanctuary, providing an escape from the challenges that surrounded her[40].

At the age of six, Oprah was reunited with her mother, but this period of her life was marred by darkness. Oprah suffered sexual abuse from multiple family members, including her uncle, cousin, and a family friend. The trauma of these experiences left lasting scars on her young mind and heart. However, Oprah's gift for public speaking began to emerge amid the darkness. She felt empowered when expressing herself and connecting with others through her words.

During her adolescence, Oprah faced another significant challenge when she became pregnant at 14. The pregnancy gave way to the birth of a baby boy; however, the unfortunate demise of the newborn occurred shortly after. This grievous defeat, in addition to the torment she sustained, caused Oprah to endure post-traumatic stress syndrome (PTSD). Despite the hardships, Oprah's father, Vernon, became a source of support and stability in her life. He pushed her to focus on her studies and nurtured her talent for public speaking[40].

Rising Stars and Breakthroughs

At 16, Oprah's life took an unexpected turn when she participated in a local radio contest called "Miss Fire Prevention" in Nashville. To everyone's surprise, she won the competition with charisma and eloquence. The victory opened a new door for Oprah as the radio station offered her a part-time job as a reporter while she was still attending high school. Balancing her studies and work, Oprah proved to be a natural in front of the microphone, captivating audiences with her voice and presence.

Oprah's talents and achievements caught the attention of local communities, and she became known as a rising star. Her brilliance shone not only on stage but also in academics. After winning Miss Tennessee beauty pageants, Oprah earned a scholarship to Tennessee State University. There, she continued flourishing as she pursued her studies and honed her public speaking skills[40].

The Oprah Phenomenon Unleashed

In 1984, Oprah's career reached a pivotal moment when she moved to Chicago to host a morning talk show called "People Are Talking." Her engaging presence and natural ability to connect with guests and audiences caught the attention of television executives. This provoked the commencement of "The Oprah Winfrey Show" on September 8, 1986. The program quickly attained success, appealing to spectators from every stratum of society. Oprah's genuine empathy, compassion, and insightful discussions endeared her to millions, making her the highest-rated daytime talk show host[41].

Oprah's tumultuous childhood experiences inspired her to make a difference in the lives of underprivileged girls. In 1997, she established the Oprah Winfrey Leadership Academy for Girls in South Africa[42]. The boarding school provided opportunities for girls from disadvantaged backgrounds to receive quality education and support. Oprah's commitment to empowering these girls stemmed from her journey of overcoming adversity and wanting to offer them a chance for a brighter future.

Inspiring Minds Through Literature

Beyond her television success, Oprah wielded enormous influence through her "Oprah's Book Club." Launched in 1996, the book club selected literary titles for viewers to read and discuss[43]. Oprah's recommendations turned unknown authors into bestsellers, sparking a literary revolution that encouraged a nation of readers. The power of Oprah's book club became so significant that being featured in it guaranteed a book's commercial success.

Business Ventures and Media Dominance

Oprah's entrepreneurial spirit extended beyond television and literature. In 1998, she invested in the Oxygen network, a cable channel designed for women. Furthermore, in 2000, Oprah launched her magazine, "O, The Oprah Magazine," which celebrated life, spirituality, culture, and more. On the 1st of January in 2011, she established the Oprah Winfrey Network (OWN), expanding her communication business to include numerous television programs and unique material[44].

Oprah Winfrey's extraordinary life journey is a testament to the indomitable human spirit and the power of transforming adversity into opportunity. From her challenging beginnings as a young girl facing hardships and abuse, she emerged as a beacon of hope and inspiration for millions worldwide. Indeed, her legacy will continue to inspire and resonate for future generations, leaving an enduring imprint of hope and empowerment on the human spirit.

Exercises For You

Empower Others Through Support

Identify a cause or community that could benefit from your support. Take actionable steps to contribute, whether through volunteering, fundraising, or raising awareness.

Start a Book Club or Reading Initiative

Initiate a book club or reading initiative within your community or workplace. Choose books that promote empowerment, resilience, and personal growth. Discuss the lessons learned with participants.

Sylvester Stallone - Journey in Bringing Rocky to Life and His Success

The name "Sylvester Stallone" has been synonymous with Hollywood for decades, particularly due to the incredible triumph of the Rocky franchise, which commenced in the 1970s. Beyond starring in these iconic films as Rocky, he also took on the roles of director and writer for a significant portion of the series. Rocky marked his initial breakthrough, propelling him into the realm of certified stardom and paving the way for numerous action-packed movies in his illustrious career. Even today, at 77, he continues to act, write, and direct films.

He journeyed from humble beginnings to achieve remarkable success, a path that was far from easy. There was a time in his life when he was utterly destitute. Sylvester Stallone found himself homeless and forced to part with all his possessions, even his beloved dog. It's heartbreaking to consider what circumstances would lead someone to sell their cherished canine companion for a mere $25. Just $25 was the amount for which Sylvester had to part with his faithful friend due to his dire financial situation![45] Like many of us might have done, he walked away from that painful moment, tears in his eyes and a heavy heart burdened by the trials he had endured. Fortunately, the legend would soon find a glimmer of hope shortly after this heart-wrenching incident.

Muhammad Ali's Bout: A Turning Point in Sylvester's Journey

Shortly after parting ways with his dog, Sylvester found inspiration in a Muhammad Ali match[46]. This newfound inspiration led him to pen a script that would mark the inception of his remarkable journey-a script that would come to be known as "Rocky." The studios were captivated by the script's potential and wasted no time offering him $300,000. Surprisingly, Sylvester turned down this generous offer, insisting on playing the leading role in the movie. However, the studios declined his proposal.

At such a crucial point in life, it's imperative to take stock of your own journey. Life calls for deliberate decisions and actions. Sylvester Stallone, a man of unwavering determination and unshakeable self-belief, is a shining example. Even during his most financially challenging times, he boldly turned down a $300,000 offer, a profoundly inspiring decision. What compelled him to make such a choice? He saw the dawning of his future, the realisation of his deepest life ambitions. At this pivotal juncture, $300,000 seemed insufficient to purchase his dreams despite his current financial constraints[47].

He later got an offer from a studio for a mere $35,000 for the script, along with the lead role in what would later become the iconic film, "Rocky." After sealing the deal, the first he did was to get his beloved dog back. To get the dog back, the new owner charged him $15,000. Some might argue it felt like a "ransom." Yet, no price was too steep for him, especially as his fortunes began to change.

The movie, produced on a modest budget of $1,000,000, skyrocketed in popularity, grossing an astounding $225,000,000[48]. Truly, a remarkable success!

Success Was No Accident for Him

Sylvester Stallone's bold decision to turn down a substantial offer for his script played a crucial role in his meteoric rise. The film "Rocky" soared to become a blockbuster, paving the way for a slew of subsequent hit movies. These are achievements Stallone says he could never have fathomed in his wildest imaginings.

His unwavering ethos of never compromising propelled him forward. His resilience, capacity to bear the hardships of poverty, and dedication to his vision made all the difference. He weathered life's blows and risked everything to achieve greatness. Fueled by a clear vision and relentless determination, he saw his dreams come to fruition and reaped immense rewards. Today, Sylvester Stallone boasts one of Hollywood's most impressive net worths and stands as one of its most iconic and celebrated actors.

8 Ways To Remain Committed To Your Dreams After Emotional Abuse

1. **Recognise The Emotional Abuse**

The first step towards healing from emotional abuse is acknowledging that it exists. This recognition is vital because it helps you pinpoint where the abuse is coming from. Sometimes, individuals may not even realise they are enduring abuse, so simply acknowledging it is a significant initial step. Emotional abuse includes behaviours such as insults, put-downs, verbal threats, or actions that make the victim feel threatened, inferior, ashamed, or degraded. It's important to note that emotional abuse can stem from both physical and non-physical actions, including instances like sexual abuse leading to emotional trauma.

2. Understand Healthy Relationships

To assess your relationships, start by understanding what constitutes a healthy one. Reflect on your romantic relationships and your interactions with family members, including maternal and paternal relationships. Do you feel safe and supported in these relationships? If you do, that's a positive sign. However, if you feel threatened or weakened around certain individuals, it may be an indicator that you need to address the situation carefully.

3. Convince Yourself

You must acknowledge whether your relationship is toxic or healthy. It should not be a challenge to recognise the nature of your relationship. Some individuals may try to cover up for their partners, relatives, or others, even going so far as to believe they deserve the mistreatment. It's important to understand that no one deserves an abusive relationship, as it can significantly impact your emotional well-being. Your dreams are as important as your health, and if your emotional stability is compromised, it can hinder your pursuit of your dreams.

4. Break The Cycle Of Emotional Abuse

Emotional abuse often follows a cyclical pattern, much like a habit, and can be broken down into four distinct stages: tension, incident, reconciliation, and calm. During the tension stage, the relationship becomes strained, leading to communication breakdown and fear. These tensions eventually erupted into a significant incident involving blaming, arguing, intimidation, and threats. Afterwards, the abuser may apologise but may still blame or downplay the incident. The final stage is often referred to as the honeymoon stage, where all issues are temporarily ignored. However, this cycle will inevitably restart with mounting tension. Whether you're currently in the honeymoon stage or not, it's crucial to recognise that the cycle will continue if not addressed.

5. Reach Out To People You Confine In

When seeking support, confide only in people you trust completely. Be cautious and discerning about who you share your experiences with. Not everyone has your best interests at heart, and some may take advantage of your vulnerability. Ask yourself, "Could this person take advantage of me? Can I trust this individual?" Remember that your goals are more important than anyone here. While working towards your goals and accomplishments, remember that not everyone can be trusted, and your dreams should remain your top priority.

6. Support Yourself

After recognising the signs of psychological mistreatment in your relationship or emotionally draining behaviour, the next step is to take action. The best way to do this is by supporting yourself. Begin by setting boundaries and clarifying what behaviours you will not tolerate, such as personal attacks. If you've been passive in the past, now is the time to be proactive. Ensure that you communicate your boundaries clearly and assertively to anyone involved.

7. Remain Confident

You should know what it takes to stand on your feet. Confidence is key to standing up for yourself and achieving your dreams. Fear and self-doubt can hold you back even if you possess all the necessary skills and resources. Who knows if confidence is the missing thing that hinders you from getting the best of yourself? How beautiful would it turn out if you worked on it today for a better tomorrow? What if the dreams lie in your confidence? If Sylvester Stallone were not confident enough, he would not have taken the courageous decision that made him a start today. You can also be a star; what if this could only be true if you forget the past and create the confidence that kills your emotional weaknesses? Yes, you can do it!

8. Reinforce Your Reasons

Continuously remind yourself why the abusive behaviour is not acceptable. As you focus on your mental health, understand why their actions and words are detrimental to a healthy relationship. Communicate to the abuser how their behaviour doesn't align with a healthy relationship and that it's affecting you negatively. If it's possible to salvage the relationship, let them know their impact on you. However, if necessary, be prepared to make the difficult decision to distance yourself from the toxic relationship.

Steven Spielberg – The Heartbreaking and Inspiring Story of the Greatest Movie Maker of All Time

"Sometimes a dream almost whisper, it never shouts. Very hard to hear. So you have to, every day of your lives, be ready to hear what whispers in your ear."

Steven Spielberg is likely a familiar name to you if you've seen any of his acclaimed films. Unknown to many, he struggled with undiagnosed dyslexia from a young age[49], facing challenges in reading and learning akin to others with the condition. Spielberg's early life was fraught with difficulties; he often felt misunderstood, with many mistaking his struggles for laziness. Peer bullying and a lack of support from educators added to his challenges. The repercussions of his disability led to a two-year delay in his educational progress. Despite receiving the same education, his peers moved ahead of him. However, Spielberg began finding solace and confidence in filmmaking during his teenage years.

Steven was resilient from a young age. Deep within, he believed in his potential; as mentioned in one of his documentaries, he felt a compelling force assuring him of his destined greatness in filmmaking. Many obstacles threatened his dreams, including a rejection from a film school. Despite being bullied, Spielberg viewed filmmaking as his anchor. He once expressed, "When I feel like an outsider, filmmaking makes me feel at home on my set."

Each of us has faced some form of bullying, either directly or indirectly. In essence, we've all encountered challenges that tempted us to surrender. Yet, many of us remained resilient, understanding that perseverance is a victory in itself. Unfortunately, not everyone manages to overcome these obstacles; some succumb to them. Regardless of past defeats or moments of surrender, it's crucial to remember that there's always an opportunity to begin anew and choose resilience once more.

Steven Spielberg: A Cinematic Odyssey

From an early age, Steven's love for cinema was incomparable. As early as fourteen years, he managed to film a short film while casting his friends and family as actors. The film's title was "Escape to Nowhere,"[50] which was recorded using his father's 8mm camera. It took him only a short time to progress with his ambition by experimenting with his crafts and shaping his experience and skills. Through his conscious and hard work, he believed and was focused on becoming a successful moviemaker.

In the early 1970s, Steven produced a suspenseful movie called "Duel," visualising a motorist chased by a cruel tanker truck. The 1971 TV movie caught the eye of Hollywood and showcased his drive towards being a progressive filmmaker. The movie provided insights into the outstanding capacity of Spielberg to build tension and suspense, which caught the audience's attention from the start to the end of the movie. The "Duel" movie was one of the special productions that started his interest and ability to indulge in the filmmaking industry. The trajectory provided insights into Steven becoming one of the most successful and influential movie directors.

Spielberg hit international recognition in 1975 through his triumph production of the "Jaws" movie[51]. The film was about a great white shark terrorising people in a small coastal town. The film not only helped Steven gain more reputation as a film producer but also proved his mastery of storytelling skills. The "Jaws" film marked a crucial turning point in Steven's movie production history. The film attracted a pool of enthusiasts excited to watch the heart-pounding suspense, creative and innovative use of animatronics, and memorable play characters.

After observing his excellence in the Jaws film, Spielberg joined the realm of science and fiction in 1982 and produced his first film, "E.T. the Extra-Terrestrial."[52] The play was a tale demonstrating a young boy's friendship with a stranded alien. The heartwarming tale touched the emotions of millions, reaffirming Steven's uniqueness and emotional reverberance. The E.T. film developed to be the most grossing of the period, demonstrating the exceptional abilities of Spielberg to actively engage characters and create a relatable play that rises beyond genre.

Based on Ballard's semi-autobiographical novel, Steven directed "Empire of the Sun" in 1987. The film concerned the acutely distressing moments of a young boy called Jim in Shanghai during World War II. The film demonstrated Steven's to draw and relate historical occurrences while elaborating on the impacts of war on children's lives. The movie led to the recognition of Steven as a creative and imaginative director with the potential to relate epic tales to character-driven narratives through the captivating performances, visuals, and storytelling observed. In 1998, he produced another film called "Saving Private Ryan", reflecting on Normandy landings during the Second World War. Spielberg's ability to demonstrate human experiences through realistic battle sequences earned him the second Academy Award as an outstanding director with the ability to tackle authenticity and empathy.

Steven Spielberg stepped to another milestone in the 1990s after venturing into the historic drama industry and producing "Schindler's List". As a professional film director, the movie showcased Spielberg's creativity, originality, and inventiveness. Based on a true story, the movie demonstrated Oskar Schindler's efforts to save the Jews during the catastrophe. The film was full of emotional scenes illustrating the terrors and panic of history with steady realism and the absolute strength behind the human spirit. The "Schindler List" film earned Steven his first Academy Award, recognising him as the best director solid in his dignitary cinemas.

Other plays produced by Steven, such as "The Terminal" in 2004, "Munich" in 2005, "War Horse and The Adventure of Tintin" in 2011, the 2012 "Lincoln" film, "Bridge of Spies" in 2015, and "The BFG" in 2016, demonstrated his commitment to engaging the audience from diversified age groups with unforgettable characters and compelling narratives. His thought-provoking themes also depict his powerful storytelling abilities, inspiring countless individuals and promoting his excellence in the film industry.

What We Can Learn From Steven Spielberg?

As a teenager, Steven embarked on a new chapter of life. His experiences serve as a guiding beacon, teaching us about the twists and turns of life. During his childhood, he faced ridicule, bullying, and emotional distress. Yet, he found a renewed sense of purpose in his teenage years, allowing him to move beyond his early adversities. While the past influences us, it doesn't define our present or determine our future. Past challenges can fuel our determination, ensuring we don't falter in similar situations again. However, if not addressed, past setbacks can also prevent us from taking new steps forward.

Each phase of our life influences the subsequent one, creating a domino effect. We can't simply "turn a blind eye" and expect to erase our past. We can either heal from our past experiences or let them burden us. To persevere, it's crucial to reflect: How has your past shaped your current journey? Has it instilled a fear of starting anew? Recognising the impact of your past on your present is essential for growth.

Emulate Steven's resilience and confront the challenges life throws at you. Steven believed filmmaking was his path to self-improvement, where he could command the narrative's direction. Yet, many doubted his choice, thinking his academic struggles would hinder his success in filmmaking. Little did they know the immense potential within Spielberg. Despite his undeniable talent, he faced rejection from film school three times in a row.

How would you react to failure at the outset? Many might lack the drive to try again, opting for a different path. But what if that new direction doesn't truly harness your potential? It's a risk. Steven likely never envisioned crowds gathering around him, eager to absorb his wisdom, or that his hardships would inspire countless others, much like the lessons in this narrative. Surrendering now means forfeiting future possibilities, sidelining the potential greatness within. Life's journey isn't linear; it can twist and turn, sometimes even redirect your aspirations. Regardless, the key is to persevere.

Steven Spielberg Achievements

- In 1987, Steven Spielberg received the Irving G. Thalberg Memorial Award for his innovative contributions as a filmmaker.

- In 1995, Spielberg was honoured with the American Film Institute AFI Life Achievement Award.

- Recognising his impactful film "Schindler's List" and his Shoah-Foundation, Steven was awarded the Federal Cross of Merit with Ribbon by the Federal Republic of Germany in 1998.

- Beyond his accolades in filmmaking, Spielberg has been knighted in both the United Kingdom and France. He was named an Honorary Knight Commander of the Order of the British Empire (KBE) by Queen Elizabeth II for his services to the entertainment industry. Furthermore, in 2004, President Jacques Chirac honored him with the title of Knight of the Légion d'honneur.

- 2006 marked another significant year for Spielberg. On July 15, the Chicago International Film Festival presented him with the Gold Hugo Lifetime Achievement Award. Later that year, on December 3, he was celebrated with a Kennedy Center honour.

- Spielberg received another Légion d'honneur accolade in 2008. That June, Arizona State University also presented him with the Hugh Downs Award for Communication Excellence.

- In 2009, Spielberg was bestowed the Philadelphia Liberty Medal, presented by former US President Bill Clinton in October.

- On October 22, 2011, Spielberg was recognised as a Commander of the Belgian Order of the Crown, the third-highest rank within the Order.

- The National Archives and Records Administration honoured Spielberg with its Records of Achievement Award on November 19, 2013.

- On November 24, 2015, former President Barack Obama awarded Spielberg the prestigious Presidential Medal of Freedom in a ceremony at the White House.

- Harvard University celebrated Spielberg's contributions by conferring upon him an Honorary Doctor of Arts on May 26, 2016.[53]

Exercises For You

Creative Problem-Solving Exercise

Spielberg's creative problem-solving is evident in his filmmaking, from "Duel" to "Jaws." Emulate his creativity by finding innovative solutions to everyday challenges in your own life.

Setbacks as Opportunities

Reflect on Spielberg's rejection from film school and how he turned setbacks into opportunities. Apply this mindset to view your own setbacks as opportunities for growth and learning.

Jay-Z's Story Gives Hope to the Hardworking

"All I got is dreams. Nobody else believes. Nobody else can see. Nobody else but me."

For anyone who has questioned how an individual can climb from nothing to international fame, the answer lies in the incredible story of Jay-Z. He has faced several challenges to demonstrate that, with enough perseverance, any goal is achievable. Simply put, Jay-Z's professional life has been a rollercoaster of successes and failures, revealing that dedication can lead to success.

Shawn Corey Carter, popularly known as Jay-Z, grew up in the Marcy Projects, a housing project in Brooklyn. His upbringing was marked by economic challenges and exposure to street life. His mother, Gloria Carter, raised him after his father left the family when Jay-Z was quite young. Despite facing financial difficulties, Jay-Z's home was filled with his mother's determination to provide for him. The Marcy Projects, while not the most affluent neighbourhood, was filled with gangs but became Jay-Z's early stomping ground, shaping his perspective on life[54].

Growing up in the Marcy Projects, Jay-Z experienced the hardship of poverty first-hand and gained a deep respect for hard work and creative problem-solving. Not only was it his home, but the community served as a network of support during times of difficulty.

Although Jay-Z was brought up in a troublesome community and had to drop his studies, his narrative shows us that our beginning does not predict where we will ultimately be. Incredibly, Jay-Z discovered he was gifted in something at a young age despite his obstacles. Numerous successful people have experienced difficult times early on; however, Jay-Z is a powerful reminder of what can be accomplished with the right mindset.

Jay-Z possessed a remarkable talent for making music, primarily rap. This insight immensely affected his life, as his ardour for hip-hop music was inexhaustible, and he was motivated to develop his ability continuously. This can be taken as a lesson for us all that no matter what obstructions may appear, if we stay dedicated and persistent, we can still reach outstanding successes.

Jay-Z's narrative exemplifies the advantages of recognising your talents and nurturing your aspirations. Growing up in a challenging environment, he chose to shield himself from negativity and embrace the positive influences around him, and this embodies Jay-Z's journey. Your background should not be an excuse to limit your future potential. Countless superstars we see today emerged from challenging beginnings, yet they steered their careers towards eventual success.

Transformation: From Passion to Dream to Opportunity

As Jay-Z grew older, his love for music became even stronger. He spent many hours writing down his thoughts and feelings in rhymes and dreaming of sharing his stories with the world. One day, he got a big chance- he met a famous music producer who saw his potential.

With time, Jay-Z started making his songs but lacked fancy equipment at first. He used his creativity to turn everyday things into beats. His friends were amazed by his talent and believed in him.

Jay-Z faced challenges, too. He was rejected multiple times by renowned record labels. However, he kept pushing forward, undeterred by these rejections. In fact, he turned his struggles to fuel his music. He shifted from just a performer to a music producer and, alongside his team, started a music label known as Roc-A-Fella Records. This was a substantial move that showcased his relentless spirit. Although some musicians left his imprint at the outset, he refused to be disheartened and saw all his issues as chances to get ahead.

By 1997, Jay-Z's determination started paying off. He did achieve his goal of releasing his music, working with other musicians like Notorious BIG, and trying other ventures. This shows us that it's important to keep trying, even when things are tough. Jay-Z didn't give up. As a result, he made important albums, like "Vol. 2 Hard Knock Life" in 1998.[54]

Jump to 2014, Jay-Z's journey was really amazing. Forbes, a big magazine, said he was one of the most important celebrities. He also became really rich, with more than $500 million[55]. This shows how smart he is about business.

But Jay-Z's influence was about more than just money. He sold more than 75 million records and won 22 Grammy Awards. This made him a big star in music. He also did something unique: he became an owner of an NBA team. This showed that he could succeed in things other than music.[56][57]

Jay-Z's journey serves as a compelling testament to the incredible resilience and determination within us all. Even when life presents its toughest challenges, we can harness our passions and channel our efforts towards success. So, dare to dream big and never cease your forward momentum. Just like Jay-Z, you possess the capacity to transform your dreams into reality, regardless of the obstacles you encounter.

When you find yourself on the brink of giving up, take a moment to look back and reflect on your journey. How far have you already come? Consider the time and effort you've invested in pursuing your dreams. Is it truly worth relinquishing now? While you may have countless reasons to throw in the towel, ask yourself if they hold more value than your hard-earned progress. Recognising where you stand amid the realms of passion, dreams, and the opportunities that await is essential.

Exercises For You

Explore New Ventures

Jay-Z ventured into music production and business. Follow his example by exploring a new venture or skill. Embrace the learning process and see how it contributes to your personal and professional growth.

Record Your Progress

Jay-Z's success is documented through record sales, awards, and business achievements. Keep a record of your own progress and achievements, no matter how small. Regularly review and update this record to acknowledge your growth.

Share Your Story

He often shares his story of overcoming challenges. Similarly, share your own story of resilience and determination with others. Your journey may inspire someone facing similar obstacles.

Dr A.P.J Abdul Kalam: A Model of Dedication and Contribution

"If you want to shine like a sun, first burn like a sun."

The remarkable journey of APJ Abdul Kalam serves as a timeless inspiration, transcending borders and generations. Renowned as a true embodiment of resilience, intellect, and humility, Dr. Kalam's biography represents the potency of willpower and relentless allegiance to one's ambitions. From humble beginnings to becoming the 11th President of India from 2002 to 2007[58], his path is an awe-inspiring narrative of a visionary, scientist, and statesman whose unwavering dedication to his country and the pursuit of knowledge continues to ignite the spark of inspiration in countless hearts worldwide.

Early Life and Education

Born into a humble family in Rameswaram, Tamil Nadu, Dr. Kalam grew up in a diverse household that fostered a profound respect for all faiths. His father, a boat owner who facilitated pilgrim transportation between Rameswaram and Dhanushkodi, faced economic challenges[59]. Despite the challenges, Dr. Kalam displayed exceptional academic prowess by dedicating himself to the field of aerospace engineering. His hard work and effort made him a respected researcher at the "Indian Space Research Organisation (ISRO) and the Defence Research and Development Organisation (DRDO)."

Dr Kalam overcame financial hardships to become an esteemed scientist and engineer, contributing significantly to India's space and defence programs. As President of India, he garnered praise for his humility, wisdom, and dedication to serving the nation. Dr. Kalam passed away in 2015, leaving a lasting legacy as a scientist, statesman, and inspirational figure for future generations.

Dr. Kalam emerged as a beacon of hope for underprivileged citizens, defying considerable obstacles to assuming the presidency. Despite his challenging journey, he consistently demonstrated compassion, generosity, and modesty to those around him.

Dr Kalam's Remarkable Dedication to Success

Dr Kalam exhibited unwavering determination on his path to success, investing over a decade of arduous work as the project leader for the indigenous Satellite Launch Vehicle at ISRO. His endless endeavours yielded one of the most paramount scientific breakthroughs in satellite deployment technology. Today, India is renowned for its profound impact in the technology field, largely owing to Abdul's contributions.

Notably, Dr. Kalam spearheaded India's inaugural satellite launch, further enhancing the nation's prestige. Despite his elevated position as the president, Dr. Kalam never considered himself superior to others and willingly relinquished power to serve the greater good.

Dr Kalam's life is captivating as he pursued his aspirations without causing detriment to those around him. While augmenting his knowledge through higher education, he faced numerous initial challenges. Dr. Kalam's life exemplifies the notion that resilience paves the way for remarkable achievements. He once profoundly stated, "A dream is not what you see when you are asleep; it is the things that keep you from sleeping." Dr. Kalam understood the profound significance of his ambitions and diligently pursued them to transform them into tangible realities.

Adding Value to His Country

While many presidents sought to acquire more from their nations than they gave, Dr. Kalam's tenure as the President of India stood in contrast. He spearheaded projects like Devil and Valiant aimed at developing long-range rockets based on the successful SLV program. Under the Kalam Mission, the rockets Agni and Prithvi, along with other initiatives, achieved significant milestones. Dr. Kalam skillfully balanced the projects he led, merging the advancements of satellite technology with ballistic missiles. His life teaches us to build upon past achievements to perfect the present ones.

Dr. Abdul Kalam was pivotal in leading the Pokhran-II nuclear tests. He served as the scientific chief under the then Prime Minister, earning him the title of the country's foremost nuclear scientist. The nuclear tests conducted under Kalam's leadership from July 1992 to December 1999 made India a nuclear-armed state[60].

Learning from Dr Kalam urges us to be mindful of the present and future. He dedicated considerable time to self-improvement and acquired knowledge to confront world challenges without faltering. Sometimes, we need to relinquish power or strength, such as through acquiring knowledge. Investing in personal growth is crucial. What skills do you need to differentiate yourself? Do you possess all the prerequisites to embark on your goals?

Despite his many accomplishments, Dr. Kalam never looked down upon anyone. It might hinder your progress if you tend to belittle people, particularly when you hold a higher position. If you refuse to give up, cultivate relationships with individuals who inspire and support your goals rather than hold you back.

Humanity Aid

Collaborating with cardiologist Soma Raju, the late president developed an innovative coronary stent called the "Kalam-Raju Stent," which contributed to making cardiac treatment accessible to all[61]. One way to attain what you desire is by sharing your abilities. Luck is not a distant concept, just as assuming responsibility is not an insurmountable challenge. Dr Kalam found fulfilment in helping others, which served as a reminder of his past struggles and fortified him to face future obstacles. Engaging in activities that evoke your past experiences can strengthen your resolve for the future. If you once faced significant debt, you can assist the less fortunate when you achieve financial stability. Such acts serve as a reminder that you were once in their shoes and motivate you to avoid a similar situation. While striving for financial stability is essential, consistently doing the same thing may not yield optimal results. Giving more to others can create a catalyst for personal growth and achieve a better version of what you desire.

5 Ways You Can Turn Failure Into Success

1. **Learn From Your Mistakes**

It's okay to make mistakes; they're not the worst thing ever. They only become a problem if you don't try to learn from them. So, always try to learn from your mistakes. Everyone makes mistakes, and that's normal. Don't stress out about it. Just remember that even the most successful people have made mistakes in the past.

2. **Proceed Cautiously With How You Converse With Yourself**

Be cautious when talking to yourself, especially when you've faced a setback. Sometimes, how you talk to yourself can be mean and make you feel bad. But don't let it make you feel worthless, especially after a disappointment. It's okay to feel hurt for a while, but then try your best to think positively and shift your focus.

3. Doing Something Imperfectly Is Better Than Doing Nothing Perfectly

The real failure is when you don't do anything because doing nothing puts everything at risk. When we don't take action, it means we're not making any progress, and that's a sure way to stay unsuccessful. All it takes for failure to succeed is for us to do nothing.

4. We Are The Results Of Our Past

We don't have to let our past mistakes define who we are. Even if things didn't go as planned in the past, we can still make our future better by thinking positively. Sometimes, we're scared to talk about our past and failures because we worry they will shape who we are. Admit your past mistakes, but focus on the good things that are yet to come.

5. The Enemy Of Success Is The Fear Of Failure

It's not failing itself that's the big problem; it's the fear of failing that makes us do nothing. To get rid of this fear, you have to face it. The best way to do that is to concentrate on what you can do, forget about what's already happened, and not be scared of failing. When you fail, you don't just lose; you also learn.

Exercises For You

Reflect on Dedication and Willpower

Consider Dr Kalam's quote, "If you want to shine like a sun, first burn like a sun." Reflect on your dedication to your goals. What sacrifices are you willing to make?

How can you channel Dr Kalam's unwavering willpower into your own pursuits?

Identify and Pursue Knowledge

Dr. Kalam's journey is marked by his commitment to education and continuous learning. Identify areas where you can enhance your knowledge to better contribute to your goals. Consider both formal education and self-improvement.

Balance Leadership and Humility

Dr Kalam, despite his elevated positions, remained humble. Evaluate your leadership style. How can you balance authority with humility in your interactions? Consider instances where you can relinquish power for the greater good.

Henry Ford: From Scratch to the Pinnacle of the Auto Industry

"Anyone who stops learning is old, whether at twenty or eighty. Anyone who keeps learning stays young. The greatest thing in life is to keep your mind young."

Henry Ford's life story poses several questions about motivation and perseverance. How strong is your motivation when it comes to chasing your dreams? Do you easily surrender when faced with challenges, or can you demonstrate determination when adversity strikes? While you might recognise Ford products as some of the world's most exceptional automobiles, the captivating narrative behind the founding of the Ford Company might be unfamiliar to you.

Early Life and Beginnings

Henry Ford initiated this company, drawing on his experience as a "watch repairman." Born on July 30, 1863, in Greenland Township, Michigan, he began his journey by repairing and reassembling watches for friends and acquaintances. This skill earned him a reputation as a watch repairman[62].

In 1876, tragedy struck as Henry Ford lost his mother, leaving him with no desire to continue working on the family farm without her. At 16, in 1879, Ford left home to become a student engineer at a boat-building firm in Detroit[63]. During his time in Detroit, he immersed himself in learning and acquiring knowledge in engineering and business. His engineering expertise led him to work as a steam engine repairer, gaining recognition even though he worked alongside notable companies like Westinghouse and Edison Electric Illuminating Company.

But Henry Ford did not stop there; he tirelessly pursued his goals while securing his daily sustenance. Henry faced numerous challenges but never considered putting his dreams on hold. Instead, he persisted in pursuing his dreams while fulfilling his responsibilities as a machine repairer.

Challenges and Learning

In due course, Henry Ford established his very own venture, the Detroit Automobile Company. Regrettably, this enterprise had to be shuttered due to the underwhelming performance of the cars it produced in the market. This initial foray into the realm of car manufacturing was marked by disappointment. While many individuals might have thrown in the towel in the face of such a setback, Henry remained undaunted. Rather than giving up, he made a resolute decision to concentrate on enhancing the quality of his vehicles. Henry thoroughly examined the root causes of his predicaments, meticulously dissecting how these failures had transpired and what had led people to hold unfavourable opinions of his cars. By delving into these inquiries, he uncovered the solutions to his challenges.

In 1901, he collaborated with the stockholders of the Detroit Company to establish the Henry Ford Company. However, shortly after its formation, he was sued by his investors and forced to leave the company. The company was subsequently renamed the Cadillac Automobile Company[64]. These two failures didn't discourage Henry but made him even more determined. He resolved to make improvements by utilising his strengths to address people's needs.

Legacy and Family Business

Henry Ford's mission extended far beyond personal success; he aimed to secure a lasting legacy for himself and his family within the business realm. Before his passing, he had amassed a substantial fortune for his family and laid the foundation for a business destined to endure through generations. This commitment has borne fruit, as the Henry Ford Company, a trailblazer in the early days of the automobile industry, continues to thrive today.

Henry's entrepreneurial journey didn't stop there. He went on to establish another venture known as "Henry Ford and Son." In a shrewd move, he showcased his unwavering commitment to excellence by ensuring that his most valuable employees joined him in this new endeavour. This strategic manoeuvre proved exceptionally successful, persuading the stockholders to relinquish their stakes, eventually rendering the Ford family the sole proprietors of the company. Henry's visionary planning was dedicated to safeguarding the family's interests, preventing a recurrence of the challenges the earlier Henry Ford Company faced.

Beyond his remarkable business sharpness, Henry Ford pioneered the concept of Welfare Capitalism, designed to benefit his workers. He revolutionised labour practices by paying his employees double the wages compared to other companies, consequently elevating the market wage rate for labourers. This pivotal shift began a significant transformation in industrial practices, where workers' well-being and fair compensation took centre stage.

Ford's commitment to his workforce extended further through the introduction of a groundbreaking 5-day, 40-hour workweek[65]. He also implemented various strategies to promote leisure, recognising its positive impact on productivity. In doing so, he reshaped the automotive industry by offering innovative, affordable cars, all while employing a large-scale production system that not only transformed the face of the automobile industry but also created a workplace centred on values and employee well-being, leaving an indelible mark on the competitive landscape.

5 Tips to Focus on Your Dream

1. **Write Down Your Goal And Stay Motivated**

Keep your goals in writing and stay motivated by reminding yourself why they matter. Let your motivation drive you towards your dreams.

2. **Find Different Sources Of Inspiration**

Use different types of inspiration to keep you going. Reward yourself when you achieve specific milestones (achievement-based inspiration), focus on the possibilities your hard work can bring (action-based inspiration), and use fear as a strong motivator.

3. **Have A Plan And Set Goals**

Create a clear plan that allows you to see how to become the best version of yourself. Avoid idleness and excuses, and make sure your ideas align with your execution pattern. Your goals, plans, and execution should work together.

4. Practice Effective Time Management

Being a good time manager is crucial for success. Build a system that helps you complete tasks on time. Don't allow room for excuses, failure, or giving up.

5. Measure Your Progress And Visualise Success

Continuously measure your progress and imagine the results of your efforts. Although the end goal is important, your present actions shape your future. Ensure your goals are measurable, and visualise the outcomes from where you start.

Exercises For You

Mastering Time Management

Improve your time management skills to optimize productivity. Develop a system that helps you complete tasks on time, eliminating room for excuses and failure. Henry Ford's efficient production systems and commitment to progress can serve as a model for effective time management.

Legacy Building

Consider your long-term goals and legacy. How committed are you to building a lasting legacy for yourself and your family? Reflect on Henry Ford's dedication to creating a family business that endures through generations and how you can incorporate such commitment into your aspirations.

Harrison Ford: Crafting Wealth from Sheer Skill

"I realized early on that success is tied to not giving up."

Harrison Ford's life journey is a source of inspiration, as it showcases the remarkable determination and talent that propelled him from an average schoolboy to a renowned Hollywood icon.

Early Life and School Days

Hailing from Chicago, Illinois, with an advertising executive father and a homemaker mother, Ford encountered various obstacles during his early years. Notably, he grappled with bullying in school, an unexpected experience that would profoundly influence his path forward. Harrison was a naturally talented student but struggled with his studies, resulting in consistent C grades.

After completing high school, Ford enrolled at Wisconsin's Ripen College, where he began to rewrite his story. Joining various clubs and taking on summer jobs, such as tree trimming, flower delivery, and assisting in the kitchen, he exhibited a strong work ethic and a willingness to learn new skills. While initially inexperienced in cooking, Ford taught himself on the job through books and diligent study. However, his low attendance and grades eventually led to the realisation that he might not graduate alongside his peers.[66]

Ford's Journey into Acting

In reaction to this setback, Ford made the pivotal choice to enrol in a drama class, signalling the commencement of his venture into the realm of acting. As he conquered his fear of public speaking and polished his acting abilities, he unearthed his passion and wholeheartedly committed himself to pursuing an acting career. While his peers veered towards conventional office occupations, Ford steadfastly adhered to his distinct life plan, with a paramount component of his aspiration to become an actor.

Upon his arrival in Los Angeles, Ford initiated a job hunt, taking on roles as a sales representative at a neighbourhood paint supply store, a rigger on a yacht, and even a late-night pizza delivery driver in Hollywood[67]. Alongside these unconventional occupations, he graced the stages of local theatre productions, catching the eye of the media. A pivotal moment came when a Hollywood writer strongly recommended Ford's meeting with a Columbia Pictures studio executive. After a comprehensive interview delving into his personal life, Ford clinched a contract with Columbia Pictures, thus inaugurating his journey as a contract player in the world of cinema.

Nevertheless, the outset of Ford's Hollywood journey proved to be a tumultuous ride. His contract with Columbia Pictures was abruptly terminated, lasting a mere 18 months, amid a dispute between him and the studio. Faced with the responsibility of supporting his growing family, Ford signed a remarkably similar contract with Universal Studios three days after welcoming his child into the world. This time, the contract placed even greater demands on him, necessitating his acting skills and his expertise as a cameraman. Despite these formidable challenges, Ford tenaciously pressed forward, accepting minor roles to secure a livelihood and provide for his family. It was an arduous period marked by adversity, yet Ford's unwavering determination remained unshaken.

At one point, Ford significantly shifted from acting to carpentry, learning the trade's intricacies. He soon found success in carpentry, even focusing on carpentry books available at the local public library[68]. His first breakthrough came when Brazilian writer-producer Sergio Mendes hired him to transform his three-car garage into a recording studio. Ford's carpentry business flourished, allowing him to be more selective with the acting roles he accepted. He managed to juggle between carpentry work and pursuing his dream of a successful acting career.[69]

Harrison Ford's Impressive Achievements

During his amazing career, Ford became really famous for his outstanding work in entertainment. He acted in some of the most famous and well-loved movies like Star Wars and Indiana Jones, which got him nominated for the Best Picture Oscar Award eight times.

Among his remarkable honours is the Albert R. Broccoli Britannia Award for Worldwide Contribution to Entertainment, presented by the British Academy of Film and Television Arts in 2015, the prestigious Cecil B. DeMille Award from the Hollywood Foreign Press Association in 2002, and the Lifetime Achievement Award bestowed upon him by the American Film Institute in 2000.

Ford's acting prowess shone brightly as he earned an Academy Award nomination for his gripping portrayal of Detective John Book in the 1985 Oscar-nominated sensation "Witness", directed by Peter Weir. Notably, he also clinched nominations for the esteemed Golden Globe and BAFTA Awards for Best Actor. What's even more impressive? Ford secured not one, not two, but three Best Actor Golden Globe nominations for his exceptional performances in Weir's 1986 drama, The Mosquito Coast; the 1994 Oscar-nominated blockbuster, The Fugitive, under the direction of Andrew Davis; and Sydney Pollack's 1996 reimagining of Sabrina.

In a significant moment of recognition, Harrison Ford was bestowed with the Box Office Star of the Century Award by the National Association of Theater Owners in 1994. This prestigious distinction stressed Ford's exceptional influence and enduring legacy within the film industry, solidifying his status as a true cinematic icon whose contributions left an indelible mark on the entertainment world.[70]

Exercise For You

Balancing Multiple Responsibilities

Assess your current responsibilities and commitments. How can you balance multiple roles, similar to Ford's juggling of carpentry work and acting pursuits? Develop strategies to efficiently manage your time and responsibilities while progressing toward your goals.

Michael Jordan: The Tale of an Iconic Legend

"I can accept failure, everyone fails at something. But I can't accept not trying."

Michael Jordan's journey to greatness had the most modest of beginnings. While his potential for greatness was evident, the means to achieve it were beyond his grasp. A young boy fueled by an unwavering passion for excellence, Jordan relentlessly pursued his dream until it became a reality. His story stands as proof of the incredible results that can be achieved through steadfast dedication, discipline, and sheer hard work.

Within each of us, unique talents are waiting to be uncovered, like hidden treasures waiting to be unearthed or, if neglected, allowed to rust away. Michael Jordan, however, refused to let his passion grow rusty, even in the face of numerous setbacks. As we delve into his remarkable journey, remember that today's failures need not define our future successes.

A Passion Ignited

Michael Jordan's affection for basketball was cultivated within the very fabric of his upbringing. With a basketball-loving father and an active-playing brother, the seeds of his love for the sport were sown early on. What began as a mere interest soon blossomed into a dream despite encountering setbacks linked to his height.[71]

High school marked the genesis of Jordan's trials, as a taller player eclipsed his position on the team. Yet, rather than succumbing to disappointment, these early setbacks ignited a fierce determination within him. His journey towards self-improvement began, and he became a living symbol of three fundamental qualities: discipline, hard work, and steadfast consistency. These qualities would remain firm companions throughout his life, accompanying him from the classroom to the courts and, ultimately, to the peak of becoming a world champion.

Overcoming Failure Through Hard Work

Failure is a universal experience, and Jordan was no exception. However, he believed that hard work could overcome any obstacle. His height and skill deficiencies were the reasons for his initial disqualification from the school team. His school coach made it clear that mediocrity was not an option, and Jordan had a limited time frame to prove himself. During his first tryout, standing at a mere five feet eleven inches, he fell short of the required height for a teenager, leading to his exclusion from the senior school team.

Undeterred, Jordan embarked on a rigorous practice regimen. He would leave home early each day, heading straight to the school sports complex to practice basketball before the first bell rang. Sometimes, the physical education teacher had to drag him to class after the bell had rung. Jordan's discipline was unwavering. Failure was no longer an option; he saw a champion within himself and tirelessly worked towards realising that vision. His dedication allowed him to enhance his skills and passion in preparation for the next tryout.

A Second Chance

When the opportunity for another tryout presented itself, Jordan seized it and secured a spot on the team. Although he mostly sat on the bench, distributing water and towels to exhausted players, he refused to lose hope. His original plan had been to become a key player on the school team, but this dream seemed distant as he found himself in a supporting role. Nevertheless, his journey of consistency continued.

Jordan eventually joined the junior school team. In his first year in the Junior Varsity division, he consistently scored twenty points per game. His coaches recognised his talent and promoted him to a higher position, where Jordan became a significant contributor. It is worth noting that if it hadn't been for his initial setback and the belief that he wasn't good enough, Jordan might never have pushed himself to excel. Jordan himself acknowledges how this early failure played a crucial role in shaping him into the remarkable person he became.

The Truth Behind Michael Jordan's Success

During the late 1980s, Jordan rose to become the biggest star in basketball, a driving force for the Chicago Bulls. His career illustrates the significance of hard work and consistency. Jordan was not necessarily the most gifted athlete in the NBA nor the most naturally talented. He faced failures but never abandoned his goals, consistently taking the necessary steps to achieve them.[72]

Michael Jordan's voyage from adversity to greatness vividly illustrates what can be achieved through resolute determination, unwavering discipline, and relentless hard work. His story serves as a compelling reminder that our present failures need not shape the course of our future successes.

5 Ways to Manage Your Time in Career Development

1. **Make Sure You Set The Right Goals**

Your goals should be clear and doable. Think of them as a kind of investment. You're putting in your money, time, and effort, hoping to get good results in the long run. Even if things don't go well right away, your goals might eventually turn out great if you keep trying hard. But they might not work out if you don't connect your goals to the things that matter most for your dreams. In this case, try using the SMART method for setting goals. That means your goals should be Specific, Measurable, Achievable, Relevant, and Time-bound. Pay attention to the timing!

2. **Smart Planning Is Important**

One way to do it is by organising your tasks properly. Sometimes, take a moment to ensure you're doing things correctly. If you work really hard, it's even better to double-check by deciding what's most important. It's not just about organising but organising things by what's really important and what needs to be done urgently. If you do this well, it will help you handle difficult situations more easily.

3. Set A Time Limit

Having a time limit is important for a better experience overall. If you go over the set time, you fall behind; if you finish before it, you exceed expectations. It helps you stay on track and be more productive. Deadlines are crucial for career development, so stick to them.

4. Get Organised And Get Rid Of Unnecessary Stuff

When you organise yourself, you make space for better time management and other activities. For instance, organising your tasks helps you see what you need to do next. It's important for a smoother experience. We all have many things to do, so create a well-organised plan. Otherwise, you might fall behind on your schedule.

5. Plan And Take Breaks When Needed

Taking breaks is important, but it won't harm you if you plan them. Working too much isn't a sign of good time management. It's when you forget to relax, which can harm you physically or in terms of productivity. Try not to take too many breaks, and convince yourself you can perform better after resting. It's important to rest your mind, even when things are tough.

Exercises For You

Dedication to Continuous Improvement

Evaluate your current approach to skill development or career advancement. Michael Jordan's commitment to continuous improvement and disciplined practice led to his success. Identify a skill or aspect of your career that requires improvement, and create a structured plan for consistent practice and enhancement.

Overcoming Self-Doubt and Persevering

Explore moments of self-doubt or feelings of inadequacy in your journey. Michael Jordan faced challenges related to height and skill, but his perseverance overcame self-doubt. Develop strategies to overcome your own doubts and build resilience, drawing inspiration from Jordan's determination.

Abraham Lincoln: The Embodiment of Resilience and Tenacity

"My great concern is not whether you have failed, but whether you are content with your failure."

An American Beacon of Hope

In the annals of American history, Abraham Lincoln stands as a shining beacon of perseverance, leadership, and vision. Though he is revered today as an iconic figure, Lincoln's path to the presidency was strewn with obstacles and personal tragedies. Yet, his enduring spirit serves as an inspiration for anyone battling life's challenges.

Humble Beginnings

Born in 1809 in a modest setting, Lincoln's early life was devoid of luxuries. His roots were grounded in a background that was far from resourceful. Despite these limitations, Lincoln's passion for learning and his insatiable curiosity set him apart.

A Series of Personal Tragedies

Life was never easy for Lincoln. In 1816, his family faced the hardship of eviction. Tragedy struck again when his mother passed away shortly after. But perhaps one of the most heart-wrenching episodes of his life was the untimely death of his first love, Ann Rutledge when he was just 26.[73][74]

Professional Struggles: A Stepping Stone to Success

Lincoln's professional journey was not without its share of setbacks. In 1831, he faced a crushing blow when he couldn't establish his business. By 1836, personal and professional stresses culminated in a mental breakdown. His political aspirations also faced numerous rejections. Lincoln confronted multiple setbacks, from losing his bid for the Illinois House of Representatives to a defeat in his aim to become the Commissioner of the General Land Office in D.C. in 1848. Yet, with every defeat, Lincoln's resilience shone brighter. As he once said, "My great concern is not whether you have failed, but whether you are content with your failure."[75]

Rising Against the Odds

While many would have been deterred by such a series of failures, Lincoln was not one to give up easily. His dedication and unwavering spirit eventually bore fruit. In 1846, he was elected to the U.S. House of Representatives, where he became a vocal advocate for ending slavery, even drafting a bill towards that aim. Then, in 1860, after years of persistence, Lincoln reached the pinnacle of his political career, becoming the 16th President of the United States.

Legacy of a Legend

Today, Abraham Lincoln's legacy is etched not only in the annals of American history but also on the U.S. five-dollar note, a testament to his enduring impact[76]. Despite countless setbacks and challenges, Lincoln's determination never wavered. His journey from humble beginnings to the White House is a testament to his incredible resilience and unyielding spirit.

A Symbol of Perseverance

Abraham Lincoln's life is more than just a story of a president; it is a tale of triumph over adversity. His journey serves as a reminder that with determination, perseverance, and belief in oneself, no challenge is insurmountable.

Exercise For You

Political Engagement and Advocacy

Assess your level of engagement in civic activities or social causes. Lincoln, despite early political rejections, became a vocal advocate for ending slavery. Reflect on your values and the causes that matter to you. Develop a plan to actively engage in or support initiatives that align with your beliefs, taking inspiration from Lincoln's commitment to social change.

Steve Jobs: The Embodiment of Technological Brilliance

"I'm convinced that about half of what separates the successful entrepreneurs from the non-successful ones is pure perseverance."

Steve Jobs, a true exemplar of self-belief and unrelenting effort, possessed a resolute vision from his earliest days. His life's narrative stands as a beacon of inspiration, illustrating the profound truth that setting early life goals and steadfastly pursuing them can lead to remarkable achievements.

Early Life and Influence of Technology

Adopted at a young age, Steve Jobs' foster parents were pivotal in moulding his character. They fostered his inquisitiveness and unveiled the marvels of technology, particularly focusing on electronics and computers. This early immersion emphasises the notion that the roots of our future passions can be planted in our youth. The obligations we bear today might very well be the stepping stones to our forthcoming accomplishments.

As Steve Jobs became captivated by the world of computers, he set forth on a path of self-discovery and education. Even in his school years, his educators discerned his extraordinary potential and proposed that he forgo certain classes, a notion his parents rejected. Rather than adhering to the conventional educational model, Jobs chose to chart his own course of exploration. This choice strikes a chord with anyone who aspires to chase their passions beyond the constraints of a classroom.

At the tender age of 13, Steve Jobs demonstrated his determination by calling Bill Hewlett, the co-founder of HP, to request electronic parts for a school project. Hewlett was so impressed that he offered Jobs a summer internship. This bold move illustrates the importance of taking proactive steps towards one's goals, even in the face of potential rejection or challenges.[77]

Challenging Formal Education

As Steve Jobs continued to grow, he developed a strong aversion to formal education. While he attended college briefly, he found little joy in it and dropped out after a semester. However, he remained committed to learning what truly interested him, such as calligraphy. This decision highlights the importance of focusing on core passions rather than conforming to societal expectations. Passion can be a guiding force, but it must be nurtured wisely to avoid investing in the wrong pursuits.

To conquer financial hurdles, Jobs sought employment at a video game company. His chief objective was to amass the funds required for his continuing education, although his pursuit took an unconventional twist. Rather than pursuing a conventional business education, he embarked on a voyage of self-enhancement. Through diligent savings, he embarked on a transformative journey to India alongside a friend. During their sojourn, Jobs delved deep into Eastern spirituality and eventually embraced Buddhism, highlighting the profound importance of personal development and the enrichment that cultural exploration can bring.

But Steve Jobs' thirst for personal growth didn't end there; he plunged into the realm of hallucinogenic substances, notably LSD, an experience he deemed one of the most profound in his life's journey.[78] These encounters etched an unconventional trajectory into his life. Jobs embraced Zen Buddhism and adopted a minimalist lifestyle in the backyard of his parents' home. This exposure to nonconformity and alternative philosophies was pivotal in sculpting his future ideas and groundbreaking innovations.

The Journey of Success

After leaving Apple, Jobs founded a new company called NeXT and developed groundbreaking software. Although NeXT initially struggled to gain traction, Apple eventually acquired it in 1996 for $429 million. Jobs' return to Apple in 1997 marked a turning point for the company. With a new management team in place and a salary of just $1 per year, Jobs led Apple to refocus on innovation. Products like the iMac received rave customer reviews, and Apple introduced revolutionary devices like the iPod, iPhone, and MacBook Air. The competition struggled to keep up, making Apple the face of innovation.[79]

In 1986, Jobs made a remarkable move by purchasing Pixar Animation Studios from George Lucas for $5 million.[80] Under the leadership of Jobs, Pixar brought forth a series of immensely triumphant movies such as Toy Story, Finding Nemo, The Incredibles, and Up. Jobs played a pivotal role in Disney's animated film achievements as well, following Pixar's acquisition by Disney in 2006 for a staggering $7.4 billion., with Jobs becoming Disney's largest shareholder.[81]

Exercises For You
Proactive Pursuit of Goals

Reflect on a goal or aspiration you have in mind. Steve Jobs, at the age of 13, proactively reached out to Bill Hewlett for electronic parts, securing a summer internship. Consider taking a bold and proactive step toward your goal, even if it involves reaching out to influential individuals in your field. Develop a strategy to initiate contact, showcasing your passion and determination.

Cultural Exploration

Evaluate the role of personal development in your life. Steve Jobs embarked on a transformative journey to India, exploring Eastern spirituality and adopting Buddhism. Consider the benefits of personal development and cultural exploration on your own growth. Explore opportunities for self-discovery, whether through travel, educational experiences, or spiritual pursuits, and outline steps to incorporate them into your life.

Balancing Passion and Pragmatism:

Analyze your approach to education and career choices. Steve Jobs dropped out of college to pursue his passions, balancing financial constraints and personal interests. Assess whether your educational and career pursuits align with your core passions. Develop a plan to strike a balance between passion and pragmatism, ensuring that your choices contribute to both personal fulfilment and practical success.

Goal-Setting Workbook: Transforming Inspiration into Action

Turning Failure into Triumph

Objective: Turn setbacks into stepping stones

Goal Identification:

Break down life goals into specific, measurable, attainable, relevant, and time-bound (SMART) objectives.

Consider short-term and long-term aspirations.

Develop a visual representation of your goals, creating a vision board for motivation.

Overcoming Obstacles:

Conduct a thorough analysis of potential challenges.

For each identified challenge, devise a detailed plan outlining mitigation strategies.

Create a contingency plan for unexpected obstacles, fostering adaptability.

Continuous Learning Plan:

Identify areas for continuous personal and professional development.

Curate a personalized learning plan with a mix of books, online courses, workshops, and mentorship opportunities.

Allocate dedicated time weekly for learning and skill enhancement.

Courage to Take Risks:

Conduct a risk-reward analysis for a specific endeavor.

Develop a risk mitigation strategy for potential negative outcomes.

Engage in a structured reflection on the perceived and actual risks involved.

Maintaining Focus:

Establish a system for goal tracking and progress evaluation.

Identify potential distractions and create a tailored plan to minimize them.

Periodically review and recalibrate goals to align with evolving priorities.

Perseverance, Confidence, and Resilience Strategy

Objective: Pursue your goals with perseverance, confidence, and resilience.

Handling Disappointment:

Create a journal for reflecting on disappointments and extracting valuable lessons.

Develop a toolkit of coping mechanisms, including positive affirmations, mindfulness practices, and gratitude exercises.

Collaborate with a mentor or support network to gain diverse perspectives.

Perseverance and Confidence:

Conduct a SWOT analysis (strengths, Weaknesses, Opportunities, Threats) for self-awareness.

Write a journal emphasizing past achievements to boost confidence.

Engage in visualization exercises to mentally rehearse overcoming challenges.

Innovations and Reinvention:

Organize brainstorming sessions to foster creative thinking.

Experiment with a small-scale innovative project to test unconventional ideas.

Seek feedback from peers or mentors to refine and iterate on innovations.

Personal Improvement

Objective: Before you can change the world, you need to take care of yourself first. After all, you can't pour from an empty cup.

Embracing Pain and Suffering:

Develop a structured self-care routine, including physical, mental, and emotional well-being.

Seek therapeutic outlets, such as counselling or creative expression, to process pain.

Establish a support network to share experiences and insights.

Navigating Relationship Changes:

Conduct a relationship audit, assessing the impact of personal connections on your creative journey.

Develop effective communication strategies for discussing changes in relationships.

Identify and nurture relationships that contribute positively to your creative endeavors.

Handling Discouragement and Jealousy:

Create a journal for documenting and reframing moments of discouragement.

Practice self-compassion and celebrate small victories regularly.

Develop a mentorship or peer-support system for shared experiences and advice.

Your Journey, Your Story: Embracing Life's Challenges with Resilience

We possess numerous belongings and experiences that we cherish daily, many of which are attained through dedication and challenges. Much like the reflections in this book, we all have stories to share about our journey. Regardless of where we are in life, it's essential to pursue genuine contentment. Possessing everything materialistic doesn't necessarily equate to happiness. It's crucial to remember that the key to a fulfilling life is to be the best version of oneself consistently. Even when faced with unforeseen hurdles, maintaining positivity and focus is vital. While our sense of happiness might fluctuate based on achievements and other factors, it's imperative to prioritise our well-being and seek joy in every circumstance.

Your accomplishments are reflections of your efforts. These triumphs aren't limited to just career or education; they can also be related to health and personal growth.

It's crucial to recognise and commend oneself, as this self-affirmation can shield against feelings of despondency and pave the way for an enriched existence. Living life fully not only enables exploration but also presents greater avenues for further success. Letting poor choices dictate the path can limit these very accomplishments. As you delve into the stories of the discussed individuals, let their experiences inspire you rather than deter you. Understand that they, too, faced hardships, much like you might be encountering now. Embrace courage and seek joy; by doing so, you'll find your path more navigable and your goals more attainable. Challenges are inevitable, but facing them with a positive mindset can make the journey smoother.

Sylvester Stallone faced immense hardships, yet he aspired for more and ultimately achieved it. He could have surrendered to his circumstances and overlooked the welfare of his beloved dog. Yet, his mental fortitude and inspiration from a fight kept him going. We all encounter obstacles and moments of despair, but taking a cue from Stallone, it's essential to find strategies and persevere rather than capitulate.

Little achievements matter. Every morning you rise is another opportunity nature grants you. Even if yesterday was challenging, today holds promise. None of the wealthy and powerful people knows what their future will be like ten years from now. You can't predict your future from here, but you can plan to give yourself the best chance possible. Giving up means limiting the possibilities for your life's potential.

Having read about the inspiring individuals in the earlier chapters, it's evident you haven't given up. Your commitment to reading this far indicates your passion and self-belief. Change is always possible; you can rise once more and create significant transformations. Your dream is still alive, and surrendering now might snuff it out! As long as you breathe, there's potential to make a difference. We all face reasons to quit-but consider Bethany Hamilton. Despite every reason to abandon her dreams after losing an arm, she persevered and fully realised them. If she can overcome her challenges, so can you. It took sacrifices and immense effort-she trained harder than most with just one arm. Yet, this wasn't a setback; it forged her into the remarkable individual she became. When faced with setbacks in life, don't be disheartened or retreat. Let the disappointment flow through you rather than holding onto it.

Instead of giving up, seek to understand the reasons behind your challenges. If you lose your job and feel all is lost, reflect on the circumstances that led to it. Everything happens for a reason, so ensure you don't give up hope without understanding.

Negativity is ever-present. If you let situations dictate, they'll shape you. If you rely too heavily on friends, they can let you down. If you yield to family pressures, they might influence you adversely. It's essential to trust in yourself. When you're on the right track, set lofty goals, envision a brighter future, and remain optimistic. True joy stems from dedication and effort. Reflect on your values, prioritise your desires, and prevent life from overwhelming you!

This book is designed to inspire and guide you on the journey you've always aspired to undertake. It's crucial to remember that each person's path is unique-so refrain from measuring yourself against others. You are singular in your existence, and your choices are your own. Strive for your personal best and resist the urge to stack yourself against others. The truest version of you is sculpted by life's myriad experiences, be they pain, anxiety, fear, or joy. Embracing these moments is essential for an authentic life. Sylvester Stallone, for instance, recalls the anguish of losing his beloved dog and facing daily challenges, yet he remained committed to his journey. His road wasn't smooth, but he persevered, ensuring his finest self emerged.

What we see on the outside is just one version of you. Your true potential lies within. It requires effort and persistence to unveil it. Only you can pinpoint that inner potential and nurture it to shine brightly.

Who could do it better? No one but you!

Who would achieve success for you? No one but you!

Who would have all the fame after success? No one but you!

ALL THE LITTLE THINGS COUNT! MAKE EACH ONE COUNT BY GIVING YOUR BEST ALL AND NEVER QUITTING!

NEVER GIVE UP!!

List Of NGO's

1. Cancer Patients Aid Association(CPAA)

The Cancer Patients Aid Association (CPAA) is a non-profit organization dedicated to supporting individuals and families affected by cancer. Founded with a compassionate vision, CPAA strives to alleviate the physical, emotional, and financial burdens faced by cancer patients. Through a range of initiatives, including medical assistance, counselling, awareness programs, and advocacy, CPAA endeavours to enhance the quality of life for those battling cancer. Their unwavering commitment and holistic approach aim to provide comprehensive support, hope, and empowerment to both patients and their loved ones on their challenging journey against cancer.

2. UN World Food Programme

The United Nations World Food Programme (WFP) stands as the world's largest humanitarian organization dedicated to eradicating hunger and ensuring food security. Established in 1961, the WFP operates on the frontlines of emergencies, conflicts, and natural disasters, providing crucial food assistance to vulnerable populations in more than 80 countries. Its multifaceted approach not only addresses immediate hunger needs but also focuses on long-term solutions, aiming to create sustainable food systems and empower communities to break the cycle of hunger and poverty. Through innovative strategies and partnerships, the WFP continues to make significant strides toward achieving a world where everyone has access to adequate and nutritious food.

3. Help Age India

HelpAge India is a non-profit organization dedicated to serving the elderly population across India. Founded in 1978, it focuses on advocating for the rights of senior citizens, providing healthcare services, creating livelihood opportunities, and offering various support programs to enhance the quality of life for the elderly. HelpAge India works tirelessly to address the unique challenges faced by older adults, striving to build a society that respects and supports its senior members.

If you would like to share your story of perseverance with us and would like to get featured on our website, get in touch with us by visiting our website www.projectnevergiveup.com.

References

1. Wayback Machine. (n.d.). https://web.archive.org/web/20220722195329/https://global.honda/content/dam/site/global/investors/cq_img/library/form_20-f/FY202203_form20f_e.pdf

2. Elizabeth Arden | Cosmetics, Beauty Products, Entrepreneur. (2023, October 14). Encyclopedia Britannica. https://www.britannica.com/biography/Elizabeth-Arden-American-businesswoman.

3. About Elizabeth Arden - Corporate. (n.d.). https://corporate.elizabetharden.com/about-elizabeth-arden/

4. Elizabeth Arden Revenue: Annual, Quarterly, and Historic - Zippia. (2023, July 21). https://www.zippia.com/elizabeth-arden-careers-22352/revenue/

5. Makeup, Skincare, Perfume & Gifts | Elizabeth Arden. (n.d.). Elizabeth Arden. https://www.elizabetharden.com/

6. Bethlehem, L. (2014, September 7). Mark Cuban: Brains and Effort Are Needed for Business, But Don't Be a Jerk - Jewish Business News. Jewish Business News. https://jewishbusinessnews.com/2014/09/07/mark-cuban-brains-and-effort-are-needed-for-business-but-dont-be-a-jerk/

7. /ccpa/. (n.d.). TribLIVE.com. https://archive.triblive.com/news/cuban-hoping-to-work-his-magic-here-someday/

8. Mark Cuban. (2023, March 15). Biography. https://www.biography.com/business-leaders/mark-cuban.

9. Jackson, A. (2023, October 21). Billionaire Mark Cuban used this sales pitch for his first tech startup in 1989—here's why it worked. CNBC. https://www.cnbc.com/2023/10/21/mark-cuban-gave-this-microsolutions-sales-pitch-in-1989-why-it-worked.html

10. HDNet to Premiere NuTech Digital Concerts. (2006, August 9). GlobeNewswire News Room. https://www.globenewswire.com/news-release/2006/08/09/346830/3419/en/HDNet-to-Premiere-NuTech-Digital-Concerts.html

11. 2929 Entertainment | Owned by Mark Cuban and Todd Wagner | Film | Movies | Magnolia Pictures | AXS TV. (n.d.). 2929 Entertainment. https://www.2929entertainment.com/

12. Keogh, J. (2022, January 17). The Truth About Katy Perry's Religious Upbringing. The List. https://www.thelist.com/735864/the-truth-about-katy-perrys-religious-upbringing/

13. Katy's bio. (n.d.). https://web.archive.org/web/20010312171856/http://www.katyhudson.com/bio.html

14. Katy Perry Named Billboard's Woman Of The Year In 2012. (n.d.). Capital. https://www.capitalfm.com/artists/katy-perry/news/billboard-woman-of-the-year-2012/

15. Microsoft Corporation (MSFT) Statistics & Valuation Metrics - Stock Analysis. (08/12/2023). Stock Analysis. https://stockanalysis.com/stocks/msft/statistics/

16. Microsoft founded. (2015, October 9). HISTORY. https://www.history.com/this-day-in-history/microsoft-founded.

17. MSN. (n.d.). https://www.msn.com/en-in/news/other/48-years-after-dropping-out-of-college-bill-gates-shares-5-things-all-graduates-should-know/ar-AA1bcf9e.

18. Bill Gates. (08/12/2023). Forbes. https://www.forbes.com/profile/bill-gates/?sh=629b0b55689f.

19. A. (2022, April 15). What is the secret to Bill Gates' success? Coding Ninjas Blog. https://www.codingninjas.com/blog/2022/04/15/what-is-the-secret-to-bill-gates-success/

20. Barney, L. (2017, July 14). Bethany Hamilton: surfing with only one arm isn't as hard as beating the stigma. The Guardian. https://www.theguardian.com/sport/2016/aug/25/bethany-hamilton-surfing-espy-award.

21. Hibler, J., & Lake, T. (2023, December 8). Bethany Hamilton | Biography, Surfing, & Facts. Encyclopedia Britannica. https://www.britannica.com/biography/Bethany-Hamilton.

22. Inspirational Story: Jim Carrey. (n.d.). Dyslexia Help at the University of Michigan. http://dyslexiahelp.umich.edu/success-stories/jim-carrey.

23. Wiki, C. T. I. (n.d.). List of awards and nominations received by Jim Carrey. Idea Wiki. https://ideas.fandom.com/wiki/List_of_awards_and_nominations_received_by_Jim_Carrey.

24. Nix, E. (2023, August 10). 7 Things You May Not Know About Walt Disney. HISTORY. https://www.history.com/news/7-things-you-might-not-know-about-walt-disney.

25. Strauss, V. (2021, November 30). Nelson Mandela on the power of education. Washington Post. https://www.washingtonpost.com/news/answer-sheet/wp/2013/12/05/nelson-mandelas-famous-quote-on-education/

26. Walt Disney's newspaper editor told the aspiring cartoonist he wasn't creative enough. (n.d.). Business Insider. https://www.businessinsider.in/19-People-Who-Found-Great-Success-After-Being-Fired/Walt-Disneys-newspaper-editor-told-the-aspiring-cartoonist-he-wasnt-creative-enough-/slideshow/24400678.cms.

27. Walt Disney's newspaper editor told the aspiring cartoonist he wasn't creative enough. (n.d.). Business Insider. https://www.businessinsider.in/19-People-Who-Found-Great-Success-After-Being-Fired/Walt-Disneys-newspaper-editor-told-the-aspiring-cartoonist-he-wasnt-creative-enough-/slideshow/24400678.cms.

28. Disneyland opens. (2009, November 24). HISTORY. https://www.history.com/this-day-in-history/disneyland-opens.

29. Meisfjord, T. (2020, March 10). Here's How Much Walt Disney Was Worth When He Died. Grunge. https://www.grunge.com/193515/heres-how-much-walt-disney-was-worth-when-he-died/

30. First billion-dollar author. (n.d.). Guinness World Records. https://www.guinnessworldrecords.com/world-records/first-billion-dollar-author.

31. J.K. Rowling | Biography, Full Name, Books, & Facts. (2023, November 9). Encyclopedia Britannica. https://www.britannica.com/biography/J-K-Rowling.

32. R. (2018, April 28). J.K. Rowling's Wizarding World was Inspired by Portugal in Surprising Ways - Portugal Tours | Ride for you Portugal. Portugal Tours | Ride for You Portugal. http://rideforyouportugal.com/2018/04/28/j-k-rowlings-wizarding-world-was-inspired-by-portugal-in-surprising-ways/

33. Shamsian, J. (2018, July 31). How J.K. Rowling went from struggling single mom to the world's most successful author. Insider. https://www.insider.com/jk-rowling-harry-potter-author-biography-2017-7#rowling-finally-signed-a-deal-with-a-small-publisher-that-made-her-pick-a-pen-name-9.

34. Harry Potter Book Awards - Harry Potter at Catch The Snitch. (n.d.). https://www.catchthesnitch.com/books/awards/

35. P. (2019, October 9). 500 million Harry Potter books have now been sold worldwide | Wizarding World. https://www.wizardingworld.com/news/500-million-harry-potter-books-have-now-been-sold-worldwide.

36. Stephen King Biography, Works, and Quotes | SparkNotes. (n.d.). SparkNotes. https://www.sparknotes.com/author/stephen-king/

37. Kennedy, M. (2019, June 20). Stephen King Recalls the Accident That Almost Ended His Life in 1999. ScreenRant. https://screenrant.com/stephen-king-near-fatal-accident-20-years-ago/

38. Romano, A. (2018, October 10). Stephen King: A guide to his horror, his history, and his legacy. Vox. https://www.vox.com/culture/2017/8/4/16066180/stephen-king-themes-cultural-influence-explained.

39. Vernon Winfrey, Oprah's father and former councilman, has died. (n.d.). Retrieved December 11, 2023, from https://edition.cnn.com/2022/07/09/entertainment/oprah-winfrey-father-vernon-dead-trnd.

40. Fry, E. (2019, August 22). A Childhood Biography of Oprah Winfrey. LiveAbout. https://www.liveabout.com/childhood-biography-of-oprah-winfrey-2535832

41. Prince, J. (2023, July 10). Oprah Winfrey Success Story: Unraveling the Icon's Journey. Seriosity. https://seriosity.com/oprah-winfrey-success-story/

42. OWLAG | Oprah Winfrey Leadership Academy for Girls. (2023, October 13). Oprah Winfrey Leadership Academy for Girls. https://www.owlag.co.za/

43. Oprah launches influential book club. (2011, March 10). HISTORY. https://www.history.com/this-day-in-history/oprah-launches-influential-book-club.

44. Oprah Winfrey's Official Biography. (2011, May 17). Oprah.com. https://www.oprah.com/pressroom/oprah-winfreys-official-biography/all.

45. Evon, D. (2015, July 22). Did a Struggling Sylvester Stallone Sell His Dog for $25? Snopes. https://www.snopes.com/fact-check/stallone-sold-his-dog/

46. Sankar, S. (2023, August 5). "Yes, I'd like to do that": Sylvester Stallone Found His 'Rocky' Inspiration in. FandomWire. https://fandomwire.com/yes-id-like-to-do-that-sylvester-stallone-found-his-rocky-inspiration-in-muhammad-alis-opponent-after-boxer-momentarily-turned-the-tide-against-boxing-legend/

47. Weisman, A. (2014, April 2). Dirt-Poor Sylvester Stallone Turned Down $300,000 In 1976 To Ensure He Could Play "Rocky." Business Insider. https://www.businessinsider.in/dirt-poor-sylvester-stallone-turned-down-300000-in-1976-to-ensure-he-could-play-rocky/articleshow/33135526.cms.

48. Rocky (1976) - Financial Information. (n.d.). The Numbers. https://www.the-numbers.com/movie/Rocky#tab=summary.

49. How Movies "Saved" Steven Spielberg From Shame. (2020, March 12). ADDitude. https://www.additudemag.com/steven-spielberg-dyslexia-hollywood-success/

50. Winfrey, G. (2016, July 29). IndieWire. IndieWire. https://www.indiewire.com/news/general-news/watch-steven-spielberg-short-war-film-escape-to-nowhere-1961-1201711398/

51. Breznican, A. (2023, July 27). 'Jaws Became a Living Nightmare': Steven Spielberg's Ultimate Tell-All Interview. Vanity Fair. https://www.vanityfair.com/hollywood/2023/07/jaws-making-of-spielberg-interview.

52. Havis, R. J., & Havis, R. J. (2018, July 27). Why E.T. the Extra-Terrestrial is Steven Spielberg's most magical film. South China Morning Post. https://www.scmp.com/magazines/post-magazine/arts-music/article/2157160/why-et-extra-terrestrial-steven-spielbergs-most.

53. List of awards and nominations received by Steven Spielberg. (2023, December 12). Wikipedia. https://en.wikipedia.org/wiki/List_of_awards_and_nominations_received_by_Steven_Spielberg.

54. JAY-Z | Biography, Songs, Empire State of Mind, Beyonce, & Facts. (2023, November 30). Encyclopedia Britannica. https://www.britannica.com/biography/Jay-Z.

55. Greenburg, Z. O. (2014, April 18). Jay Z's Net Worth: $520 Million in 2014. Forbes. https://www.forbes.com/sites/zackomalleygreenburg/2014/04/18/jay-zs-net-worth-520-million-in-2014/?sh=9494fb557f6e.

56. Greenburg, Z. O. (2019, June 3). Artist, Icon, Billionaire: How Jay-Z Created His $1 Billion Fortune. Forbes. https://www.forbes.com/sites/zackomalleygreenburg/2019/06/03/jay-z-billionaire-worth/?sh=552a56263a5f.

57. M. (2004, August 12). It's Official: Jay-Z Is A Part-Owner Of New Jersey Nets. MTV. https://www.mtv.com/news/mqj6fv/its-official-jay-z-is-a-part-owner-of-new-jersey-nets.

58. DR. A.P.J. Abdul Kalam | President of India. (n.d.). https://presidentofindia.nic.in/former-president/dr-apj-abdul-kalam.

59. Saifi, T. (2023, February 21). jainulabiddin marakayar | Father of A.P.J Abdul Kalam. TS HISTORICAL. https://www.tshistorical.com/jainulabiddin-marakayar/

60. V. S., & V. S. (2023, August 24). Dive Into The Pivotal Moments That Have Defined India's Journey Into Space. Homegrown. https://homegrown.co.in/homegrown-voices/dive-into-the-pivotal-moments-that-have-defined-indias-journey-into-space.

61. A. (2015, July 29). Kalam-Raju stent--Missile Man's invention saved many lives | TheHealthSite.com. TheHealthSite. https://www.thehealthsite.com/news/kalam-raju-stent-missile-mans-invention-saved-many-lives-po715-314796/

62. Gauge, Used by Henry Ford for Watch Repair, 1876-1878 - The Henry Ford. (n.d.). https://www.thehenryford.org/collections-and-research/digital-collections/artifact/17317/

63. A Young Henry Ford - The Ford Story - Henry Ford Heritage. (2016, March 16). Henry Ford Heritage Association. https://hfha.org/the-ford-story/young-henry-ford/

64. HENRY FORD BIOGRAPHY. (n.d.). Retrieved December 12, 2023, from https://corporate.ford.com/articles/history/henry-ford-biography.html

65. Henry Ford started the 40-hour workweek but the reason will surprise you. (2017, July 27). India Today. https://www.indiatoday.in/education-today/gk-current-affairs/story/40-hour-workweek-henry-ford-1026067-2017-07-27.

66. Wisconsin Life: https://wisconsinlife.org/story/han-solo-in-ripon-harrison-fords-wisconsin-roots/

67. Harrison Ford. (n.d.). https://ganeshyamalabittu.tripod.com/heroes/id38.html.

68. INC. (n.d.). Retrieved December 13, 2023, from https://www.inc.com/jeff-haden/harrison-ford-is-perfect-example-of-why-you-should-hang-on-to-your-full-time-job-while-you-start-your-new-business.html.

69. Bergren, J. (2023, August 25). FLASHBACK: The Surprising Story Behind Harrison's Ford Viral '70s Carpenter Photo. Entertainment Tonight. https://www.etonline.com/news/221373_the_story_behind_harrison_s_ford_viral_carpenter_photo.

70. I. (n.d.). Harrison Ford. IMDb. https://www.imdb.com/name/nm0000148/awards/

71. Burgess, J. (2023, February 22). When did Michael Jordan start playing basketball? - Sports Nostalgia HQ. Sports Nostalgia HQ. https://www.sportsnostalgiahq.com/when-did-michael-jordan-start-playing-basketball/

72. Michael Jordan | Biography, Stats, & Facts. (2023, November 17). Encyclopedia Britannica. https://www.britannica.com/biography/Michael-Jordan.

73. Brown, K. B. (2023, December 13). Ann Rutledge: Abraham Lincoln's First True Love? History Cooperative. https://historycooperative.org/ann-rutledge-and-abraham-lincoln/

74. Whitworth, E. (2023, October 30). Abraham Lincoln's Early Life: 1809-1829 (And There Was Light). Shortform Books. https://www.shortform.com/blog/abraham-lincolns-early-life/

75. Mikkelson, D. (2000, July 11). Did Abraham Lincoln Endure Failure Before Presidency? Snopes. https://www.snopes.com/fact-check/abraham-lincoln-failure/

76. Program, U. C. E. (n.d.). $5 Note. U.S. Currency Education Program. https://www.uscurrency.gov/denominations/5.

77. Psychology Today. (n.d.). Retrieved December 13, 2023, from https://www.psychologytoday.com/us/blog/adoption-diaries/201503/adoption-in-the-life-of-steve-jobs.

78. A quote by Steve Jobs. (n.d.). https://www.goodreads.com/quotes/542554-taking-lsd-was-a-profound-experience-one-of-the-most.

79. Dormehl, L. (2022, December 20). Today in Apple history: Apple brings back Steve Jobs with NeXT buyout | Cult of Mac. Cult of Mac. https://www.cultofmac.com/459054/apple-buys-next/

80. Laman, L. (2023, July 31). We Actually Have George Lucas and Steve Jobs To Thank for Pixar. Collider. https://collider.com/george-lucas-pixar-steve-jobs/

81. The Visionary Behind Pixar: Steve Jobs. (n.d.). Retrieved December 13, 2023, from https://shrek-movies.com/the-visionary-behind-pixar-steve-jobs/

www.ingramcontent.com/pod-product-compliance
Lightning Source LLC
LaVergne TN
LVHW061547070526
838199LV00077B/6936